A DICTIONARY OF
JAPANESE FOOD

INGREDIENTS and CULTURE

RICHARD HOSKING

TUTTLE Publishing

Tokyo │Rutland, Vermont│ Singapore

"Books to Span the East and West"

Tuttle Publishing was founded in 1832 in the small New England town of Rutland, Vermont [USA]. Our core values remain as strong today as they were then—to publish best-in-class books which bring people together one page at a time. In 1948, we established a publishing outpost in Japan—and Tuttle is now a leader in publishing English-language books about the arts, languages and cultures of Asia. The world has become a much smaller place today and Asia's economic and cultural influence has grown. Yet the need for meaningful dialogue and information about this diverse region has never been greater. Over the past seven decades, Tuttle has published thousands of books on subjects ranging from martial arts and paper crafts to language learning and literature—and our talented authors, illustrators, designers and photographers have won many prestigious awards. We welcome you to explore the wealth of information available on Asia at **www.tuttlepublishing.com**.

Published by Tuttle Publishing, an imprint of Periplus Editions (HK) Ltd.

www.tuttlepublishing.com

© 1995 (text and drawings) by Richard Hosking
All rights reserved.
LCC Card No. 96-60572
ISBN 978-4-8053-1335-0

First edition, 1996

Line drawings by Richard C. Parker
Printed in Malaysia

DISTRIBUTION

Japan
Tuttle Publishing
Yaekari Bldg., 3F, 5-4-12 Osaki
Shinagawa-ku, Tokyo 141-0032
Tel: (81) 3 5437 0171
Fax: (81) 3 5437 0755
sales@tuttle.co.jp
www.tuttle.co.jp

North America, Latin America & Europe
Tuttle Publishing
364 Innovation Drive,
North Clarendon, VT 05759-9436
Tel: 1 (802) 773 8930
Fax: 1 (802) 773 6993
info@tuttlepublishing.com
www.tuttlepublishing.com

Asia Pacific
Berkeley Books Pte. Ltd.
3 Kallang Sector #04-01
Singapore 349278
Tel: (65) 6741-2178
Fax: (65) 6741-2179
inquiries@periplus.com.sg
www.tuttlepublishing.com

27 26 25 24 23   10 9 8 7 6 5   2306VP

To my father
FRANK
for his ninetieth birthday
with love and gratitude

Contents

Foreword 7
Preface 11
Introduction 13
    Pronunciation of Japanese   14
    Japanese Writing   14
    Arrangement of the Dictionary   15
    Scientific Names   16
Japanese-English 17
English-Japanese 163
Appendices:
     1 Chopsticks   183
     2 Katsuobushi   185
     3 The Kitchen and Its Utensils   187
     4 Kombu   190
     5 The Meal   193
     6 Miso   196
     7 Saké   198
     8 Salt   200
     9 Sansai   202
   10 Soy Sauce   204
   11 Sushi   206
   12 Tea   208
   13 The Tea Ceremony   210
   14 Umami and Flavor   211
   15 Vegetarianism   216
   16 Wasabi   218
   17 Wasanbon Sugar   219
Recommended Reading 221
Works of Reference 223

Foreword

I first came to Japan as a student where, living with a Japanese family, I began to absorb the rhythms of everyday life—especially the rhythms of the kitchen with its aromas and flavors. My introduction to Japanese food began—quite literally—by learning to eat fish and soup for breakfast. In subsequent years I returned to Japan often and, after living there for eleven fascinating years, now count it as a second home.

My love of Japanese cooking has traversed every stage of my adult life—as a college student, as a young mother with infant child, as a mom with a growing family, and as an empty nester. It has been a decades-long learning experience. Along the way I studied Japanese cooking with Michiko Odagiri, Japan's Julia Child, and for a year, weekly, with another cooking teacher in her apartment kitchen, learning *katei ryoori*—home style cooking. All along the way I was constantly cooking with Japanese friends. Even with this background, my copy of Richard Hosking's wonderful book was never far from my side and served as an invaluable companion—whether I was preparing nabe in Tokyo or bento in Boston. As a food writer for *The Boston Globe*, I often write about japanese cuisine and culture and find this book to be a great reference source. When I finally sat down to write *My Japanese Table: A Lifetime of Cooking with Friends and Family* (Tuttle, 2011), Hosking was again always at my side.

There has been an explosion of interest in Japanese cuisine and an unanticipated number of cookbooks have appeared in English since the late 1990s when Hosking first published his wonderful dictionary. Japanese restaurants have expanded beyond the hip urban centers and sushi has become available in supermarkets worldwide. From Boston to Berlin, Japanese cuisine has progressed beyond teriyaki and sukiyaki. Thanks to anime and manga, food that once was the exclusive province of academics or international travelers is now available to mass publics and people of every age around the world.

Hosking is himself an accomplished scholar. And, as you will discover, even though his explanations go beyond what you normally find in the glossary of a cookbook, they all are eminently accessible. Even the occasional esoterica, like his explanation of making the traditional Japanese sweet wasanbon sugar, is engaging.

A Dictionary of Japanese Food, *Ingredients & Culture* packs a powerful, but compact punch. In the hands of a different author, the volume and quality of information would require triple the amount of space—and likely also the price. Interspersed with the facts are Hosking's personal opinions and philosophy of food and culture, obtainable only by one who has become intimate with daily life in Japan after living and working there for 25 years.

Ever the purist, Hosking avoids including some Japanese comfort food staples like *kare* rice (curry rice), a Japanese adaptation of a British adaptation of Indian cuisine that is uniquely Japanese and enjoyed by everyone in Japan. But, as he explains, his book is not about food that is eaten in Japan, it is about *Japanese* food.

This dictionary is a treasure trove of information for serious home cooks, professional chefs, travelers, restaurant goers, and dabblers in Japanese culture generally. It takes you to places you didn't know you wanted to go—but will be very glad to have visited, including the whys and the science of Japanese food.

For example, I learned long ago how to make *dashi*, the smoky Japanese bonito fish stock that is the underpinning for most soups and sauces in Japanese cuisine, from scratch. I was taught how to soak the *konbu*, and scatter the *katsuboshi* flakes in the just boiled water. But I didn't know why this combination was so important.

Hosking explains that the chemical reaction which occurs between the ingredients are what creates the desired result. I love learning something new, and it happens every time I open this book.

The appendices contain supplementary explanations on topics or ingredients in need of greater detail like the tea ceremony and the family meal. His entry on *umami*, the savory fifth taste—discovered in Japan and another element of Japanese cuisine that has seeped into food talk far from Japan's shores—is priceless.

The list of Japanese ingredient names that no longer need translation is much longer today than when Hosking compiled his original list. Words like edamame, wasabi, udon and nori no longer need translation these days as they have become a part of our culinary vocabulary.

This is no simple dictionary. In describing fish for sashimi or for grilling, Hosking tells you everything about it from the waters of its origin to its proper dimensions. But he does not merely pair words with descriptions. In his discussion of wasabi, for example, you learn not only about how and where it grows (in the shade and water of mountains)—but also how to process it and with what kind of grater as well as how it is used, mixed with soy sauce for dipping; he also alerts us to the contents of cans of wasabi powder and tubes of wasabi paste, so readily available and widely used both inside and outside of Japan.

Hosking's pedagogy takes many forms, including entries that appear as romanized Japanese words as well as in kanji and one of the two Japanese syllabaries, hiragana or katakana. There is also a section that takes the reader from English to Japanese, so you can quickly learn that abalone is *awabi* in Japanese. He reaches beyond food to explain table settings, to unpack the constitution of a meal, what is *obento*, and even to introduce quirky eating establishments such as Japan's ubiquitous *akachochin*, the tiny informal drinking establishments signified by a red lantern hanging at the entrance.

The presentation and appearance of Japanese food is of supreme importance. Indeed, one often hears the Japanese say that "we eat with our eyes" (*me de taberu*). Hosking explains that the way the Japanese meal looks—its careful arrangement on plates according to colors and seasons—is as important as the way it tastes. The reader learns along the way that cooking Japanese is more than simply a matter of following a recipe but is a method of carefully crafting a presentation.

There are no recipes in this book. But once you start cooking Japanese cuisine at home, you will reach for it again and again. In closing, a phrase used by the Japanese at the beginning of a meal, seems most appropriate here—*"Itadakimasu!"*

—Debra Samuels
Boston, Massachusetts
July 2014

Preface

I was ordered to write a book on Japanese food by Dr. Max Lake, the great Australian authority on wine and food. But it wasn't until Nicholas Ingleton, president of Charles E. Tuttle Publishing Company, invited me to write this dictionary that I had the possibility of obeying the order. It has given me enormous pleasure and stimulation to do so.

Several people have helped me greatly and I wish to give them my sincerest thanks.

Caroline Davidson, my agent, got the project started by introducing me to Nicholas Ingleton and has kept me going with valuable advice ever since. Yokichi and Hiroko Okamoto have constantly helped and stimulated me with their invaluable friendship and their remarkable knowledge of Japanese food. Richard C. Parker produced his delightful, extremely appropriate line drawings at short notice. Richard B. Parker and Patricia have sustained me with their constant encouragement and enthusiasm for the project. Above all, my old friend and mentor, Professor Naomichi Ishige of the National Museum of Ethnology, Osaka, has kept a watchful eye on this effort and has made many valuable corrections and suggestions, for which I am deeply grateful.

I owe a special debt of gratitude to Hiroshima Shudo University, which has employed me for the last twenty-two years. Not only has the university encouraged me by putting me in charge of graduate-school teaching in food anthropology, but also I was given six months' leave to work on this book at the National Museum of Ethnology. Former dean Masayuki Ishiguro has been especially helpful.

Finally, I wish to acknowledge the immense value of the *Chōri yōgo jiten*, a most remarkable dictionary of cookery terms, with its eight hundred contributors and 1,275 pages. Published by the Zenkoku Chōrishi Yōsei Shisetsu Kyōkai, it is a mine of useful and interesting information, which the Japanese are indeed fortunate to have. I have not hesitated to seek in it an authoritative source of the information I needed.

Hiroshima

Introduction

This is a dictionary of Japanese food, not a dictionary of food eaten in Japan. That is an important distinction that highlights the way the Japanese observe a strict distinction between Japanese style and Western or other style. Green tea is Japanese and is drunk out of Japanese-style handleless cups. Coffee is Western and is always drunk out of Western-style cups. Green tea appears in this book, coffee does not (except in passing). Curry rice, one of the most popular dishes in Japan, is not considered Japanese and therefore does not warrant an entry.

The approach of this book is that of a non-Japanese living in Japan, and the book is intended to be a help to other such people, as well as to any other speakers of English wishing to know about Japanese food. There is a great need for accurate information on this subject in English. In Japanese, a large number of excellent books is readily available, so the Japanese and those who can read Japanese are already well catered for.

There are some excellent books in English that give the background and context of Japanese food and eating. Donald Richie's *A Taste of Japan* is first-rate. My favorite book on Japanese food is Mitsukuni Yoshida's *Naorai: Communion of the Table*. Details of these and other useful books in English can be found in the list of Recommended Reading on pages 221. There is also a list of the Japanese books that have been valuable sources of reference on page 223.

Pronunciation of Japanese

All of the Japanese words that appear in this dictionary have been transliterated in Roman letters, basically according to the Hepburn system, which is practical rather than scientific. The important point to remember is that Japanese is spoken evenly in equally stressed syllables, as in Hi-ro-shi-ma and To-yo-ta. The syllables usually consist of a consonant followed by a vowel. There is never a consonant at the end of a syllable. You will often see *n* at the end of a syllable, but this indicates nasalisation of the preceding vowel and *n* is not a consonant in this case. A macron above a vowel, i.e., ‾, indicates that the vowel is long and should be lengthened in speech. In certain positions, unvoiced consonants become voiced. The *s* of sushi becomes *z* in *nigirizushi*. Similarly, *k* can become *g*, *t* can become *d*, and *h* can become *b*. For more specific information on Japanese pronunciation, readers should consult pages 13 through 19 of Carolyn R. Krouse's *A Guide to Food Buying in Japan*, a most useful book.

Japanese Writing

There are three different scripts used for writing Japanese, and these are mixed together as needed. Two of the scripts, *hiragana* and *katakana*, are syllabaries. In this dictionary I give all native Japanese words in *hiragana*, and words of foreign origin are written in *katakana*. The third script is the Chinese script, which in many ways is more definitive than the syllabic writing, so I have tried to give the Chinese characters wherever possible. Some of those given are extremely rare and unusual, and therefore in my view all the more worth presenting.

Arrangement of the Dictionary

The dictionary is arranged in three parts: Japanese-English, English-Japanese, and Appendices.

The Japanese-English section is the part of the dictionary where almost all the details are given. The heading of an entry is always a Japanese word given in transliteration and printed in boldface. Certain Japanese words, such as sushi, tofu, and tempura, have become accepted as English. But as a heading, tofu becomes **tōfu** and tempura becomes **tenpura**. I extend this to kombu, which as an entry heading is **konbu**. Following the Romanized forms are written Japanese forms for recognition and identification. The scientific names of animals and plants are also important for correct identification, and these too, checked in Japanese sources, are included. Many of these names are hard to find and perhaps because they are in Latin, seem to get misspelled very easily. Even important publications are full of mistakes in this respect.

Cross-references are indicated by a boldface entry. Thus, **shiso** in the body of an entry means that there is a separate entry devoted to *shiso* that can be consulted. Some entries include cross-references to the Appendices.

The English-Japanese section is primarily a selective index to the Japanese-English section, which is referred to by the use of boldface. However, also included are some commonly used food items not found in the Japanese-English section, for example, bread and loaf of bread. Words that are the same or very similar in both languages, words like banana, butter, cheese, chocolate, and tomato, are generally not included in the dictionary.

The Appendices provide information in a more discursive way on topics that the reader should find interesting. Appendix 9, Sansai, is an exception, since it is a list of mountain vegetables.

Scientific Names

Scientific classification has always involved differences of opinion, quite apart from agreed changes. So I have tried to follow the best Japanese sources, which, for example, prefer *Prunus* to *Armeniaca* as the name of a genus, and *campestris* to *rapa* as a species of *Brassica*.

My experience writing this book suggests that scientific names are the cause of more headaches than anything else in this world!

There is no way that a book of this size could encompass the whole breadth of something so rich, extensive, and imaginative as the Japanese cuisine. Those who criticize the Japanese for lack of imagination should try a top-class *kaiseki* meal. The imaginative artistry of the chefs is quite extraordinary. All this book attempts to do is to provide basic and, I hope, accurate information. The only real way to understand Japanese food is to eat it, preferably in Japan.

Japanese–English

Notes: Boldface indicates the heading of an entry and acts as a cross-reference to another entry in the Japanese-English section. Italics is used for foreign words, chiefly Latin names, Japanese words that are not main entries, and for second mention of main-entry terms. In the few cases where a Japanese name follows a Latin one, the Japanese name appears in roman, e.g., *Conger myriaster* (ma-anago) in the **anago** entry.

—A—

abekawamochi あべかわもち 安倍川餅 grilled cut **mochi** topped either with sugar and **kinako** mixed, or with syrup and then *kinako*.

abura-age あぶらあげ 油揚げ thin deep-fried sliced tofu. An essential ingredient of **inarizushi**.

aburana あぶらな 油菜 rape *Brassica campestris* var. *nippo-oleifera*. Most important for the oil obtained from its seeds (**natane**) but the leaves are also used as a green vegetable.

aemono あえもの 和え物 a cooked salad, one of the basic categories of Japanese cuisine. Cooked vegetables such as spinach are dressed with a thick dressing such as sesame paste gently flavored with soy sauce and sugar (*goma ae*). *Hōrensō no goma ae* (spinach dressed with sesame), although simple, is one of the outstanding dishes of Japan. Tofu and miso are also used for dressings.

agari あがり 上がり freshly drawn tea, short for *agaribana* 上がり花. Above all, a sushi-shop term.

agedashi あげだし 揚げ出し deep-fried food such as tofu, **nasu**, and whitefish eaten with soy sauce seasoned with grated ginger and grated **daikon**.

agedashidōfu あげだしどうふ 揚げ出し豆腐 tofu from which much of the moisture has been pressed is coated with **katakuriko** or wheat flour, deep-fried, sprinkled with **katsuobushi** shavings, and served with grated ginger and **daikon** in a soy-based sauce such as **warishita**.

agedōfu あげどうふ 揚げ豆腐 thick deep-fried sliced tofu used in soups, **nimono**, and many other ways.

agekamaboko あげかまぼこ 揚げ蒲鉾 a special kind of **kamaboko** that is deep-fried. It is called **satsuma-age** in the Tokyo region.

agemono あげもの　揚げ物　deep-fried food, the best known of which are tempura, **kara-age**, and **furai**.

ainame あいなめ　鮎魚女、鮎並　fat greenling *Hexagrammos otakii*. A fish found in rocky-shore areas. When very fresh, this soft-fleshed fish can be served as sashimi. Otherwise, it is prepared as teriyaki, **nitsuke**, or **chirinabe**.

aji あじ　鯵　jack, horse mackerel *Trachurus japonicus*. A true jack, this delicious and very popular fish attains a length of up to 30 cm and is available all year but is at its best from spring to autumn. It is served as sashimi, **shioyaki**, **sunomono**, and **nitsuke**.

ajinomoto あじのもと　味の素　brand name for the chemical seasoning monosodium glutamate as marketed by the Ajinomoto company. *See also* Appendix 14 for monosodium glutamate.

ajishio あじしお　味塩　salt mixed with a chemical seasoning, usually monosodium glutamate. *See also* **ajinomoto**.

ajitsuke あじつけ　味付け　seasoning, flavor added in some way.

ajitsuke nori あじつけのり　味付け海苔　seasoned laver. *See also* **nori**.

akachōchin あかちょうちん　赤堤灯　unpretentious drinking shop displaying a large red paper lantern outside as a kind of pub sign.

akadashi あかだし　赤出し　**miso shiru** made with **akamiso**, in particular **hatchō miso** and other all-soybean misos.

akagai あかがい　赤貝　cockle, ark shell, blood clam *Anadara broughtonii*. This clam can reach a diameter of 12 cm and is at its best in spring. The freshest ones are eaten raw with a dipping sauce of soy sauce and **wasabi**, or **sanbaizu**. They are also served on sushi, put into soups, prepared as **namasu**, **nitsuke**, and **yaki-mono**, and can be baked in the shell.

akajiso あかじそ　赤紫蘇　red perilla. *See also* **shiso**.

akamiso あかみそ　赤味噌　*See* Appendix 6.

akebi あけび　木通、通草　akebi *Akebia quinata*. An autumn fruit, fairly insipid though it can be sweet. The outer shell is purple and the shape of a huge pea pod. Rarely seen in shops.

amadai あまだい 甘鯛 tilefish (a kind of sea bream) *Branchiostegus japonicus*. The flesh of this food fish of western Japan is somewhat watery.

amaebi あまえび 甘海老 pink shrimp, northern shrimp *Pandalus borealis*. *See also* **ebi**.

amaguri あまぐり 甘栗 *See* **kuri**.

amai あまい 甘い sweet.

amami あまみ 甘味 sweetness. As one of the five basic tastes, the word is usually pronounced **kanmi**. *See also* **kanmi**.

amanatsu あまなつ 甘夏 common name for the orange-type citrus fruit *kawano natsu daidai* かわのなつだいだい 川野 夏橙 *Citrus natsudaidai*. It is a variety of **natsumikan** that ripens earlier (in February and March) and is less sour than other varieties.

amazake あまざけ 甘酒、醴 a hot drink made by mixing cooked rice with water and rice **kōji** and holding at from 50 to 60°C for between twelve and twenty-four hours. It is sweetened and often flavored with ginger, and is particularly drunk for colds and sore throats and on New Year visits to shrines and temples. A quicker but inferior version is made from **sakekasu**.

ame あめ 飴 candy, toffee, a kind of **higashi**. *See also* **mizuame**.

ami あみ 醤蝦、海糠魚 opossum shrimp, mysis *Neomysis* spp. An extremely small shrimp, not longer than 2 cm at the most. It is usually made into **shiokara**, but is also dried and prepared as **tsukudani**.

amiyaki あみやき 網焼き grilling done on a griddle (*yakiami*). *See also* **yakimono**.

an あん 餡 paste made from starchy pulses and sugar and mostly used as a filling for **wagashi**. The commonest type is red and made from **azuki** and can be either sieved as *koshian*, or unsieved as *tsubuan*. **Shiroan**, which is off-white, is made from white kidney

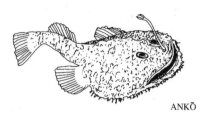

ANKŌ

beans. It can also be made from potatoes, sweet potatoes, chestnuts, and lily roots.

anago あなご 穴子 conger eel *Anago anago* (goten-anago) and
Conger myriaster (ma-anago). This sea eel can reach up to 90 cm
in length, but is usually taken at 30 to 40 cm. At its best in July
and August, it makes wonderful **nigirizushi** and is also prepared
as **kabayaki**, tempura, **nabemono**, **sunomono**, **chawan mushi**,
and **mirinboshi**.

ankake あんかけ 餡掛け sauce made by mixing **kuzu** flour or **katakuriko** with water or vegetable stock and heating till it thickens.

ankō あんこう 鮟鱇 angler fish 1. *Lophiomus setigerus* 2. *Lophius
litulon*. A fearsomely ugly but excellent tasting fish that grows
from 1 to 1.5 m and is at its best in winter. A favorite way of eating it is simmered in **warishita** as *ankōnabe*. It is also made into a
soup with red miso. The liver is served in vinegar.

anmitsu あんみつ 餡蜜 **mitsumame** with **an**. A sweet dish popular at **kanmidokoro**.

anzu あんず 杏子、杏 apricot *Prunus armeniaca* (rather than
Armeniaca vulgaris "*ansu*"). Excellent apricots are grown in the
Japan Alps, but they are not readily available, especially in the
warmer parts of Japan, and most of the crop is made into apricot
jam. For the Japanese apricot, *see also* **ume**.

aojiso あおじそ 青紫蘇 green perilla. *See also* **shiso**.

aonori あおのり 青海苔 green laver *Enteromorpha*. *See also* **nori**.

aoyagi あおやぎ 青柳 *See* **bakagai**.

aradaki あらだき 粗炊き a simmering of large fish, usually such fish as **tai** or **buri** that is not fresh enough to be eaten as sashimi or grilled. The head and the body still with its bones are simmered in stock flavored with soy sauce, saké, sugar, and **mirin**. Vegetables such as **gobō** are sometimes added.

arai あらい 洗い a style of sashimi in which slices of fish are washed in cool water, then plunged into iced water for a minute, and drained. It is a particularly useful treatment for fish such as **koi** that might have a muddy taste.

arame あらめ 荒布 arame *Eisenia bicyclis*. A non-cultivated seaweed that is dried in the wind. It must be harvested young and is tasty when fried or cooked with rice or with other foods.

arani あらに 粗煮 *See* **aradaki**.

arare あられ 霰 little rice crackers resembling hailstones. They are eaten with drinks as **tsumamimono**.

asakusanori あさくさのり 浅草海苔 purple laver *Porphyra tenera*. *See also* **nori**.

asanomi あさのみ 麻の実 Indian-hemp seeds *Cannabis sativa*. These sterilized seeds of marijuana, all imported, are not at all narcotic. They do not taste of much either, but are traditional in the seven-spice mixture **shichimi tōgarashi**, for which they are parched and added whole to the mix.

asari あさり 浅蜊、蛤仔 short-necked clam *Tapes philippinarum*. These clams are eaten from winter to early spring but should never be eaten in late spring or summer. Nor should they be eaten raw. They are served in the shell in **miso shiru**, and the flesh is served as **tsukudani**, **sunomono**, **kakiage**, and in **zōsui**.

asatsuki あさつき 浅葱 asatsuki chive *Allium ledebourianum*. Very similar to **nira** and **wakegi**, it is shallow-fried as a vegetable, used in **nabemono**, and as an herb flavoring with sashimi of **fugu** (*fugusashi*).

AWABI

atsuage あつあげ 厚揚げ thick sliced tofu fried briefly in very hot oil so that the inside remains unchanged. With **abura-age** the slices are thinner and fried right through. *Atsuage* can be eaten on its own with soy sauce flavored with ginger, and is also served as **nimono**, **itamemono**, **aemono**, and **o-den**. It is also called *nama-age*.

awa あわ 粟 foxtail millet *Setaria italica*. Along with **hie**, foxtail millet used to be eaten by poorer Japanese as a cheap substitute for rice. It is grown in Kyushu and Shikoku and may be cooked on its own or mixed with rice. It must be eaten hot, since it goes hard when cold. It is made into millet cakes (*awa-mochi*), millet balls (*awadango*), and millet candy (*awa-ame*).

awabi あわび 鮑 abalone *Nordotis* spp. A favorite but expensive shellfish. Live, it is eaten raw as sashimi, its crisp chewiness being highly appreciated. It is also steamed, boiled, and cooked as **ishiyaki**. At its best in May and June.

awasemiso あわせみそ 合わせ味噌 a mixture of different kinds of miso. It is considered to make the most delicious miso soup.

ayu あゆ 鮎 sweetfish *Plecoglossus altivelis*. A river fish growing up to 30 cm in length but usually 12 to 15 cm on the market. It is caught between June and August, traditionally with trained cormorants and flares at night. Drinking parties are held on board the fishing boats, with the *ayu* out of the cormorants' throats straight into the eaters' mouths via the grill. Today it is mainly caught by rod and line or trapped. *Ayu* has a particularly good flavor and is usually grilled as **shioyaki** and served with *tade su* as a dip. The late-season fish, *ochiayu*, heavy with roe, is considered the tastiest.

BAI

azuki あずき 小豆 azuki (adzuki, aduki) bean (pronounced a zoo key) *Vigna angularis*. A little red bean of which the Japanese are especially fond. It is an ingredient of **sekihan** and from the earliest times has been cooked with rice. **An**, the sweet paste used as a filling for many Japanese cakes and confections, is mostly made from *azuki* and sugar, which are also ingredients for **shiruko**.

—B—

bai ばい 蛽、海蠃 a species of whelk *Babylonia japonica* Family Buccinidae. This kind of whelk, also called *baigai*, is from 7 to 10 cm in length, in girth about 7 cm. The flesh is removed from the shell, boiled, and made into **sunomono**, **aemono**, and **tsukudani**.

baikingu ryōri バイキングりょうり バイキング料理 buffet. In 1958 the Imperial Hotel in Tokyo opened a smorgasbord restaurant. This buffet style of food service has come to be known as *baikingu*, the Japanese pronunciation of viking, through association with the Swedish smorgasbord. Very popular for receptions at hotels, which often also serve breakfast in this way.

bai niku ばいにく 梅肉 sieved flesh of **umeboshi**. Used as a topping and a dip, it has sharp, salty flavor that offsets bland foods such as tofu. It is sold in bottles.

bakagai ばかがい 馬鹿貝 hen clam, surf clam, round clam *Mactra chinensis*. Similar in shape and size (4 cm wide, 6.5 cm thick, and 8.5 cm long) to the **hamaguri** clam, this shellfish is widely distributed throughout Japan. It is eaten as sashimi, **sunomono**, and **kakiage**. The red peduncle is also eaten as sashimi and **sunomono**. *Baka* means fool, and since many object to the use of such a term, *bakagai* is sometimes called *aoyagi* 青柳, after a village in Chiba Prefecture where it is taken in abundance.

bancha ばんちゃ　番茶　common green tea. *See also* Appendix 12.

barazushi ばらずし　ばら鮨　*See* Appendix 11.

bareisho ばれいしょ　馬鈴薯　*See* **jagaimo**.

ba sashi ばさし　馬刺　horse-meat sashimi *Equus caballus*. A specialty of Kumamoto and Nagano prefectures, horse meat is sliced thinly and served raw with garlic and ginger-flavored soy sauce.

bateira ばていら　馬蹄螺　turban shell *Omphalius pfeifferi*. A conical-shaped shellfish about 5 cm tall and 5.5 cm round. It is tasty when boiled and served as **sunomono**, **aemono**, or **nimono**.

battera バッテラ　from Portuguese *bateira*, meaning boat-shaped. A specialty of Osaka, this sushi is made in a special wooden box in which sushi rice is pressed with vinegared mackerel topped with a transparently thin slice of **konbu**. *See also* **saba-zushi**.

benishōga べにしょうが　紅生姜　*See* **shōga**.

benitade べにたで　紅蓼　water pepper *Polygonum hydropiper* forma *purpurascens*. Also called *murasakitade*, the extensively cultivated little purple leaves have a peppery flavor. They are often placed next to the **wasabi** for mixing with soy sauce as a dip for sashimi. Parched **tade** is used as a garnish for soups.

benizake べにざけ　紅鮭　sockeye salmon, red salmon *Oncorhynchus nerka*. A northern Pacific fish of 50 to 60 cm in length, it mostly comes to Japan frozen. The bulk is salted and sold for grilling. It is also used in Western-style cooking.

bentō べんとう　弁当　boxed meal consisting of rice, pickles, and any number of accompanying foodstuffs. Most *bentō* are prepared at home to be taken to school or the workplace for lunch. There is also a large industry preparing and selling *bentō* at all times

BIWA

of day or night, often with the rice put in hot at the time of sale. There are also restaurants, especially in Kyoto, that specialize in *bentō*, which may extend beyond the box and not actually be portable. Perhaps the best-known kind of *bentō* is the *ekiben* えきべん 駅弁, sold at all major railway stations throughout Japan, usually with some distinct local touch. **Makunouchi bentō** まくのうちべんとう 幕の内弁当 is a good standard *bentō*, while *shōkadō bentō* しょうかどうべんとう 松花堂弁当 is high class and elegant.

bera べら 遍羅、倍良 Family Labridae includes a large number of very colorful fish, especially *sasanohabera* (*Pseudolabrus japonicus*), and several kinds of wrasse called *kyūsen*. As well as being the basic ingredient of **kamaboko**, it is prepared as **nitsuke**, **kara-age**, and **nanbanzuke**. Also called **gizami**.

bettarazuke べったらづけ べったら漬け **daikon** pickled in **kōji**. It has a sweet flavor and alcoholic aroma. Highly recommended.

biifun ビーフン 米粉 Chinese rice noodles. Popular in Japan, but not strictly part of Japanese cuisine.

biwa びわ 枇杷 loquat, Japanese medlar *Eriobotrya japonica*. A very bland, early-summer fruit, eaten fresh. It may also be canned, and used in jams, jellies, and liqueurs.

bōfū ぼうふう 防風 1. common abbreviation of **hama bōfū**. 2. root of *Ledebouriella seseloides*, one of the ingredients of **toso**.

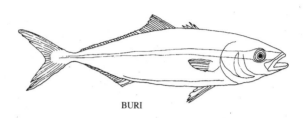

BURI

bora ぼら　鯔、　鯉 striped mullet, (British) grey mullet *Mugil cephalus cephalus*. Growing up to 80 cm in length, this fish is suitable for sashimi only when extremely fresh, since it feeds on mud and green algae and deteriorates very quickly. It is best eaten as *gyoden* ぎょでん　魚田 (fish **dengaku**), teriyaki, or **misozuke**. The female roe of *bora* is made into **karasumi**. *See also* **chinmi**.

botan ebi ぼたんえび　牡丹海老 botan shrimp *Pandalus nipponensis*. *See also* **ebi**.

botan nabe ぼたんなべ　牡丹鍋 **nabemono** with wild boar (**inoshishi**) as the main ingredient. *Botan* is Japanese for peony.

budō ぶどう　葡萄 grape *Vitis* spp. Eaten fresh in late summer and autumn, the best grapes are a considerable luxury. There is a vigorous wine industry in Japan, and though the number of discriminating consumers is increasing, they tend to prefer imported wines.

buntan ぶんたん　文旦 pomelo, shaddock *Citrus grandis*. The largest of the citrus fruits, it is grown in Kyushu and Shikoku. It is eaten raw and is similar to the grapefruit, though not as juicy. The candied peel is a popular delicacy. *Buntan* is also called **zabon**.

buri ぶり　鰤 yellowtail, Japanese amberjack *Seriola quinque-radiata*. A large fish about 1.3 m in length and weighing about 15 kg, it is highly regarded and is particularly good as sashimi and also very good grilled and as teriyaki. It is at its best in autumn and winter and is extensively cultivated artificially, as is its younger form (**hamachi**). In western Japan, *buri* is the favored fish at New

Year. It is first eaten as sashimi, then in **zōni**, later grilled, especially as teriyaki, and finally fixed as **aradaki**.

buta niku ぶたにく 豚肉 pork *Sus scrofa* var. *domesticus*. Pork is principally eaten as **tonkatsu**, but also appears in **yakiniku** and **nimono**.

butsugiri ぶつぎり ぶつ切り roughly chopped fish or meat on the bone, though fish may be filleted. It is mostly used in soups and **nabemono**.

—C—

cha ちゃ 茶 tea *Camellia sinensis* (otherwise *Thea sinensis*). Introduced from China at the end of the sixth century, Japanese tea is green tea, *ryokucha* りょくちゃ 緑茶, a term that indicates the leaves are dried without fermentation. This is achieved by sterilizing the leaves with steam before they are dried. They may be powdered for making **matcha** for the tea ceremony, or infused with hot (rather than boiling) water, in one of several grades. The best is **gyokuro**, next is **sencha**, and the ordinary tea for daily use is **bancha**, which, when freshly toasted, becomes **hōjicha**. *See also* appendices 12 and 13.

chabudai ちゃぶだい 卓揪台 low table used without chairs for serving food and drinks in a Japanese-style room. Such tables have been used only since the beginning of the Meiji era (1868) and at first were often round. The legs are often collapsible for convenience of storage. The word *chabudai* is rather old-fashioned, being largely replaced by *zataku*.

chāhan チャーハン 炒飯 Chinese-style name for **yakimeshi**.

cha kaiseki ちゃかいせき 茶懐石 the highly refined style of food associated with the tea ceremony. Since it is not desirable to drink strong **matcha** on an empty stomach, the practice arose of serving a meal beforehand. The menu should emphasize the season, and is based on rice with **ichijū sansai**. The meal starts with a tray of rice, soup, and **mukōzuke**, followed by *wanmori* (the *cha kaiseki* term for **nimono**) and **yakimono**. *Hashiarai* (a clear **suimono** soup to "wash the chopsticks") is then served with *hassun*, usually two **chinmi**, one from the mountains (e.g., **iwatake**) and one from the sea (e.g., **karasumi**). Finally, **kō no mono** is served with *yutō* (hot washings of the rice pot served in a *yutō*, a lacquerware container shaped like a teapot without a handle).

chankonabe ちゃんこなべ ちゃんこ鍋 **nabemono** that is supposed to fatten up sumo wrestlers. Basically a kind of **mizutaki**, it consists of soup made with roughly chopped chicken on the bone, in which seasonal vegetables, chicken, fish, and tofu are cooked and then dipped in a mixture of soy sauce and vinegar flavored with finely sliced **negi**. Traditionally the flesh of quadrupeds was not used, since being down on all fours means defeat in sumo. However, in recent years this custom has not been strictly observed.

chanpon チャンポン 1. a famous local dish of Nagasaki. A selection of pork, squid, prawns, oysters, and fish is fried in ample lard along with thinly sliced onion, carrot, cabbage, and other vegetables, and is then served in a large bowl containing lightly cooked Chinese noodles and soup made from roughly chopped pork and chicken on the bone. 2. the practice of mixing Japanese and Western drinks during the same drinking session.

chasen ちゃせん 茶筅、 茶筌 delicate bamboo whisk used for making **matcha**. These whisks are a special product of the town of Takayama in Nara Prefecture. There are also electric ones for people with weak wrists.

chāshū チャーシュー 叉焼 sliced roast pork served with **rāmen**.

chawan ちゃわん 茶碗 bowl, usually made of china or pottery for serving food, especially rice, and **matcha**.

chawan mushi ちゃわんむし 茶碗蒸し steamed savory custard made of egg and **dashi**. It usually contains chicken, prawns, gink-

CHIMAKI

go nuts, **kamaboko**, **yurine**, and **mitsuba**, and is steamed in special china cups with lids. Well-liked by all.

chikuwa ちくわ 竹輪 paste of fish (**surimi**), starch, and egg white, with salt, sugar, and other seasonings, formed into sausage shapes on skewers, and steamed or grilled. Among many uses, it makes an agreeable **tsumamimono**.

chimaki ちまき 粽 **mochi** made of glutinous or non-glutinous rice or rice flour wrapped in bamboo leaf and steamed or boiled. It is particularly eaten on Boys' Day, May 5, because of its phallic symbolism. May 5 is now usually called Children's Day.

chingensai チンゲンサイ 青梗菜 pak choy rape, bok choy *Brassica campestris* var. *chinensis*. Useful all-purpose green vegetable of Chinese origin, it is boiled or sautéed.

chinmi ちんみ 珍味 rare and unusual food, or food regarded as a great delicacy or luxury, such as **uni**, **konowata**, and **karasumi**, the "three great *chinmi*" (*tenka no sandai chinmi* 天下の三大珍味) of the Edo period (1603–1868).

chinpi ちんぴ 陳皮 dried peel of citrus fruit such as **mikan**, **daidai**, or **yuzu**. It is an ingredient of **shichimi tōgarashi**.

chinu ちぬ 茅渟 black bream *Acanthopagrus schlegeli*. *See also* **kurodai**.

chirashizushi ちらしずし 散らし鮨 *See* Appendix 11.

chirimenjako ちりめんじゃこ 縮緬雑魚 small young sardines and especially anchovies, less than 3 cm long, called *shirasu* in eastern Japan. After they are boiled and then dried, they are called *chirimen* in western Japan and **shirasuboshi** in eastern Japan. They

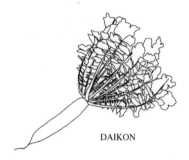

DAIKON

can be made into **aemono** with grated **daikon**, and provide a good dietary source of calcium.

chirinabe ちりなべ ちり鍋 **nabemono** in which fish, tofu, and vegetables are simmered in water and then eaten after being dipped in a mixture of soy sauce and vinegar. A popular winter dish.

chirirenge ちりれんげ 散り蓮華 china spoon. *See also* **renge**.

chisha ちしゃ 萵苣 lettuce *Lactuca sativa*. Refers mainly to a small, flat-leaved, non-heading lettuce. Otherwise, the word *retasu* レタス is used.

choko ちょこ small pottery vessel for drinking saké. *Choko* is a variant of *choku* 猪口, meaning wild boar's mouth, which a *choko* is said to resemble when viewed from the side.

chōmiryō ちょうみりょう 調味料 condiment, seasoning. The main ones are salt, pepper, mustard, **wasabi**, sugar, vinegar, stock, chemical seasoning (i.e., monosodium glutamate), soy sauce, miso, and Worcester sauce.

chōrishi ちょうりし 調理師 licensed chef.

chōshoku ちょうしょく 朝食 breakfast. A traditional Japanese breakfast consists of rice, **miso shiru**, and **tsukemono**, with toasted **nori**, egg (usually raw, to be broken onto the rice or into the soup), fish, and **tsukudani**.

chūkasoba ちゅうかそば 中華蕎麦 another name for **rāmen**, it also refers specifically to Chinese noodles.

chūshoku ちゅうしょく　昼食　midday meal, lunch. Less formal words for lunch are *hiru gohan* and *hiru meshi*, *hiru* meaning midday.

chūtoro ちゅうとろ　中とろ　*See* **toro**.

—D—

daidai だいだい　橙、回青橙　bitter orange, Seville orange *Citrus aurantium*. An important part of the New Year decoration. The juice of this orange is mixed with soy sauce to make the superior dip **ponzu** for **nabemono**.

daidokoro だいどころ　台所　kitchen. *See also* Appendix 3.

daikon だいこん　大根　giant white radish *Raphanus sativus*. Usually about 35 cm long, it is an important item in the Japanese diet, and is prepared in many ways. Thick slices are served boiled in stock with other vegetables as **nimono**. Dried in long thin strips, it is called **kiriboshi daikon** and, when reconstituted, has many uses, such as in **fukujinzuke**. Grated, it can be eaten with a flavoring of soy sauce and is added to the dip for tempura because it helps the digestion, especially of oily foods. It can be quite pungent and also unpleasantly smelly if left around after preparation. An old name for *daikon* as one of the *haru no nanakusa* (seven herbs of spring) is **suzushiro**.

daizu だいず　大豆　soybean *Glycine max*. Extensively used in Japanese food, it is highly nutritious, being a very good source of protein. Soybeans are eaten straight from the boiled pods (**edamame**) as **tsumamimono**, and removed from the pods are added to many dishes and soups. They are also used in the manufacture of tofu, miso, and soy sauce, and the parched beans are used to make **kinako** flour, a very tasty topping for **mochi**. Good-quality cooking oil is also extracted from soybeans.

DATSU

dango だんご 団子 ball (of food). The flours of rice, wheat, buckwheat, and millet are all used to make balls that are steamed or boiled and then served with some topping or dipped in soy sauce and grilled. Pork, beef, chicken, and fish (especially sardine) balls may be deep-fried instead of steamed or boiled and are often an ingredient of **o-den**.

dashi だし 出し、 出汁 stock. The best Japanese stock is made with freshly shaved **katsuobushi** and **konbu**. The first brew (*ichiban dashi*) is used for **suimono**, then the same ingredients can be reused to make "second-run" stock (*niban dashi*), which is perfectly satisfactory for miso soup, noodle broth, and many other uses. The little dried anchovies called **niboshi** are also used for making stock, but first their heads should be removed and discarded.

dashijiru 出し汁 *See* **dashi**.

datemaki だてまき 伊達巻き rolled omelet. Eggs, shredded whitefish, **dashi**, **mirin**, and sugar are used to make an omelet, which is rolled by means of the special bamboo mat called a **makisu** and then cut into thick slices. It is especially used at New Year as part of **o-sechi ryōri**.

datsu だつ 駄津 needlefish *Strongylura anastomella*. Similar in appearance to **sayori**, this sea fish reaches 1 m in length and is mostly used for making **kamaboko**.

demae でまえ 出前 home delivery of food ordered by telephone. A popular practice in Japan.

denbu でんぶ 田麩 flesh of whitefish and shrimp that has been boiled, shredded, parched, seasoned, and colored red. It is used as

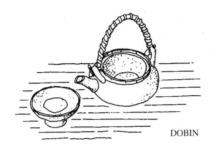

DOBIN

an ingredient of **norimaki** and as a topping for **chirashizushi**. It is also called **oboro**.

dengaku でんがく　田楽　preparation in which food such as eggplant, taro, **konnyaku**, and tofu are dressed with a sweetened miso topping and grilled on skewers. Fish *dengaku* is called *gyoden*.

denpun でんぷん　澱粉　starch ($C_6H_{10}O_5$). It is used in the making of **kamaboko** and in some preparations of **mizuame**, **nori**, and saké.

dobin どびん　土瓶　teapot. Made of pottery or china, it has a semicircular bamboo handle over the top.

dobinmushi どびんむし　土瓶蒸し　delicate clear soup made in an individual miniature **dobin**. It is a famous autumn speciality of Kyoto and usually contains **matsutake**, chicken, **mitsuba**, and **ginnan**. The juice of **sudachi** is squeezed into the **dashi**, which is drunk from little cups. The other ingredients are fished out with chopsticks and eaten. One of the great delicacies of Japan.

doburoku どぶろく　濁醪、濁酒　*See* Appendix 7.

dojō どじょう　泥鰌　loach *Misgurnus anguillicaudatus*. A freshwater fish that used to proliferate in rice paddies before the extensive use of agricultural chemicals. Since the whole fish is eaten, it is a good source of calcium. It is usually eaten as an accompaniment to **shōchū** or saké. Not highly rated.

DOJŌ

donabe どなべ 土鍋 earthenware pot, shaped like a large bowl, much used for **nabemono**. Usually its lid has a hole in it and it is glazed inside but not out. For cooking, it is placed directly on top of a **konro** or **shichirin**.

donburi どんぶり 丼 1. pottery or china bowl, two or three times the size of a rice bowl, often with a lid. 2. the food served in such a bowl, consisting of rice with various ingredients placed on top. Among the favorites are **oyako donburi**, in which chicken and egg are used, **tendon** with tempura, **gyūdon** with beef, **katsudon** with **tonkatsu**, and **unadon** with eel. These dishes provide a simple, popular meal in a bowl.

dotenabe どてなべ 土手鍋 **nabemono** in which the stock is richly flavored with miso. The usual ingredients are oysters and **yakidōfu**, with **shirataki** and a variety of fresh vegetables.

—E—

ebi えび 海老、蝦 prawn, shrimp *Penaeidae* spp. The word *ebi* covers a wide range, including crawfish (**ise ebi**), but unqualified, it usually refers to prawns or shrimps, of which there are many varieties. The **amaebi** is a sweet-tasting prawn about 12 cm in length particularly used for sushi. The **kuruma ebi** is larger, at up to 20 cm, and is used for sushi even more than *amaebi*. It is also used for sashimi and **agemono**, the best example of which, deservedly very popular, is *ebi furai*, in which these succulent large prawns are coated with egg and bread crumbs and deep-fried. For tempura, the popular prawn is *saimaki ebi*, about 7 to 10 cm long, but also the larger *shiba ebi*, 10 to 15 cm, is extensively used. *Shiba ebi* is particularly tasty and is also used in sushi, **sunomono**, and **kakiage**. The **botan ebi** grows to 14 cm and is in season from October to May. It can be eaten raw and is also prepared as tempura and **furai**. The **hokkai ebi**, about 13 cm long, is prolific off the northern shores of Hokkaido. It can be prepared as **tsukudani**, though much of the catch is peeled and canned. The giant among the prawns is the **taishō ebi**, 27 cm long. A kind of **kuruma ebi**, its true name is *kōrai* (Korean) *ebi*. It is used for tempura and **furai** and is good sautéed with vegetables. At the other end of the scale, the **sakura ebi** is a pretty little shrimp of 5 cm, a light red color and highly luminescent. It can be eaten as is, but is usually dried, either in the sun or with applied heat. It is used to provide a colorful touch.

edamame えだまめ 枝豆 pod soybean *Glycine max*. In summer, pods of young soybeans (**daizu**) on the stalk are boiled and the beans eaten as a side dish with beer. Also called **sayamame**.

edomaezushi えどまえずし 江戸前鮨 *See* Appendix 11.

egoma えごま 荏胡麻 perilla *Perilla frutescens var. frutescens*. The leaves are used in the same ways as those of **shiso**, and the seeds, when parched, smell just like **goma**. An edible oil (*eno-abura*) is also made from the seeds.

ei えい 鱝、鱏 skate, ray Order Rajiformes. The wings of these large fish, up to 2 m in length, must be eaten very fresh. Skate is cooked as **nimono**, especially **misoni** (*nimono* with miso flavoring) and *ei no nikogori* 鱝の煮凝り, in which the simmered skate is cooled and jellied. It is also made into *amazuankake*, a kind of **ankake** with sweetened vinegar.

ekiben えきべん 駅弁 boxed lunch sold at a railway station. All the major railway stations (*eki*) throughout Japan have for sale their own special boxed lunch. *See also* **bentō**.

ENOKITAKE

endō えんどう　豌豆　peas *Pisum sativum*. Green peas, although they have been grown in Japan for a long time, are not greatly used in traditional Japanese cooking. A favorite use is to mix them with mashed potato as a salad.

enokitake えのきたけ　榎茸　winter mushroom *Flammulina velutipes*. The heads of these tiny white mushrooms on long, thin stalks, growing in clumps, would average about 1 cm. They are very versatile in use, but are mostly eaten in **nabemono**.

—F—

fu ふ　麩　wheat gluten. This ancient product for which Kyoto is renowned comes in two forms. One is raw gluten (*nama fu*). A dough is made from strong flour (high-gluten flour) and water, and the starch is washed away by kneading under water. The resulting sticky substance is almost completely protein. Usually glutinous rice flour or some other flour is incorporated and coloring as desired. It is then steamed. *Nama fu* is made into all sorts of decorative shapes and has an important place in **shōjin ryōri**, being used in clear soups and **nimono**. The other *fu* is *yaki fu*, for which *nama fu* is grilled or dried in a wide variety of shapes and sizes. It is used in soups, **nimono**, and **sunomono**.

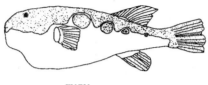

FUGU

fucha ryōri ふちゃりょうり　普茶料理　vegetarian cuisine of Chinese-style Zen Buddhism. In Japan it is practiced by the Obaku sect of Zen, centered at Manpuku-ji, the great temple at Obaku, near Uji. This vegetarian cuisine is also served at smaller temples and convents in Kyoto and other places. *See also* Appendix 15.

fugu ふぐ　河豚　puffer, blowfish Family Tetraodontidae. The various kinds of *fugu* are best known for their poison, and perhaps the main reason for dining at a *fugu* restaurant is the uncertainty and excitement that this knowledge arouses in anticipation. Certainly the taste of the fish itself is not sufficiently enticing to make one want to take the risk. *Tora fugu* is considered the best, and can weigh up to 2.5 kg. The restaurant preparation of *fugu* is very strictly controlled, but domestic preparation, whether of *fugu* caught on a fishing expedition or bought in a fish market, leads to deaths from time to time. Many, including myself, have survived eating the liver, which is the tastiest and also the most poisonous part, though it has been illegal to serve the liver since 1984. *Fugu* is served as sashimi and **chirinabe**, and the fins are toasted and hot saké poured over them. This saké is usually drunk as an aperitif.

fuka ふか　鱶　another word for shark, especially the larger species. The shark's fin of Chinese cooking is *fukanohire* ふかの ひれ　鱶 の鰭. Most species of shark are called **same** in Japanese.

fuki ふき　蕗　Japanese butterbur, sweet coltsfoot *Petasites japonicus*. Looking like giant rhubarb, the 1.2-m-long stems of this veg-

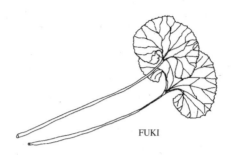

FUKI

etable have a slight flavor of celery. They are blanched and peeled before being fried or made into various pickles. *Fuki* is also candied. There is a giant variety with 180-cm-tall stalks.

fukinotō ふきのとう 蕗の薹 unopened bud of Japanese butterbur. Available only in early spring, the buds are blanched to remove some of the bitterness and are used in **miso shiru**, tempura, **tsukudani**, and **nabemono**.

fukujinzuke ふくじんづけ 福神漬け one of the most popular pickles and an invariable accompaniment of Japanese-style curry and rice. A mixture of seven vegetables thinly sliced is salted and then pickled in soy sauce and **mirin**. The seven vegetables are chosen from among white radish, eggplant, lotus root, ginger, **shiso** buds, turnip, **shiitake**, **udo**, sword beans, **shirouri**, and others.

funa ふな 鮒 wild goldfish *Carassius auratus*. A freshwater fish mainly found in lakes such as Lake Biwa near Kyoto, famous for its *funa* called *nigoro buna* (*C. auratus grandoculis*), which is made into *funazushi*, an ancient form of sushi. *Funa* lives for ten to fifteen years, reaches a length of 40cm, and is at its best in winter. It is used for **narezushi**, sashimi, **sunomono**, **tsukudani**, and in soups. *See also* **narezushi**.

furai フライ a very popular method of cooking in which prawns, fillets of fish, or slices of meat are dipped in egg, coated with **panko**, and deep-fried. *Ebi* (prawn) *furai* is a particularly successful dish.

furikake ふりかけ 振り掛け topping sprinkled on hot rice. Usually it contains toasted seaweed and sesame seeds as well as ground dried fish and salt.

furofuki ふろふき 風呂吹き winter dish in which well-boiled white radish or turnip is served with a topping of miso flavored with **yuzu** or sesame. The classic dish is made with **daikon**.

—G—

ganmodoki がんもどき 雁擬き tofu product. Tofu is mixed with crushed **yamanoimo** and chopped vegetables such as carrot, **shiitake**, and burdock, as well as sesame seeds, ginkgo nuts, and kelp. This mixture is formed into balls, the size and shape largely depending on local custom, and deep-fried. The balls are used in **o-den** and **nimono**.

gari がり thinly sliced ginger macerated in sweetened vinegar. *Gari* is served as a condiment in sushi shops, and the word is special sushi-shop vocabulary.

gazami がざみ 蝤蛑 blue crab *Neptunus trituberculatus*. *See also* **watarigani**.

genmai げんまい 玄米 brown rice *Oryza sativa*. Few Japanese eat brown (i.e., unpolished) rice, with the result that it is not easy to get hold of. Best cooked in a pressure cooker, even though the latest rice cookers claim to do the job.

genmai su げんまいす 玄米酢 brown-rice vinegar. An excellent, high-class vinegar, often made by the traditional methods. Best of all is glutinous brown-rice vinegar (*genmai mochigome su*). Not readily available, it has such an elegant sweetness and smoothness that it can be drunk neat.

geso げそ 下足 squid tentacle, cuttlefish tentacle. Often sold from stalls at festivals as teriyaki, these tentacles are also dried for use

GINNAN

GOBŌ

as **tsumamimono**. *Geso*, a shortened form of *gesoku* げそく　下足, which means footwear, was originally a sushi-shop word that has spread into common parlance.

gindara ぎんだら　銀鱈 sablefish *Anoplopoma fimbria*. A kind of cod that grows to almost 1 m in length, this fish comes frozen to Japan from the Bering Sea. It is delicious and can be cooked in numerous ways but spoils quickly and should be cooked and eaten as soon as thawed.

ginnan ぎんなん　銀杏 ginkgo nut *Ginkgo biloba*. The fruit of this lovely and very primitive tree (*ichō* in Japanese), though not strictly nuts, do have a shell that must be cracked to get at the kernel. Gathered in September and October, they are yellowish green and about 1.5 cm long out of the shell. Perhaps at their best when skewered and grilled, they are also a regular and welcome ingredient of **chawan mushi**.

gizami ぎざみ *See* **bera**.

gobō ごぼう　牛蒡 great burdock, edible burdock *Arctium lappa*. It is only in Japan that burdock root is eaten as a vegetable, usually about 1 m long and 3 cm thick. In China it is used as a medicine. The root is a very good source of dietary fiber and nutrients and should be scrubbed rather than peeled, since much of the flavor is close to the skin. For use, it is shaved (like a pencil is sharpened, *sasagaki* in Japanese) and dipped in cold water with a little vinegar to remove its considerable bitterness, because of which it is unsuitable for **nabemono**. Burdock is combined with carrot to make **kinpira gobō** and is used in **kakiage** and numerous other dishes.

gogyō ごぎょう 御形 cudweed *Gnaphalium affine*. Better known as *hahakogusa* ははこぐさ 母子草. *See also* **nanakusagayu**.

gohan ごはん 御飯 cooked rice. As with the informal word **meshi**, it can also refer to a meal.

goma ごま 胡麻 sesame *Sesamum indicum*. A nutty-flavored, oil-rich little seed of which three forms are marketed: black, white, and golden. Golden sesame has the best aroma but is not so readily available. Sesame is always parched before being used in such things as in **furikake**, **aemono**, and **goma dōfu**. Sesame oil is used in cooking, particularly for its flavor, and is important in the oil mixture for tempura.

goma dōfu ごまどうふ 胡麻豆腐 sesame tofu. Rather like a firm, baked, savory custard only gray, this resembles tofu only in texture and presentation. White sesame, usually parched, is pulverized with water, and the liquid is strained. This liquid is thickened with **kuzu** and set in a square shape. Served with **wasabi**, it can be highly recommended. Sesame tofu has an important place in all schools of Buddhist vegetarianism, such as **shōjin ryōri** and **fucha ryōri**.

goma shio ごましお 胡麻塩 sesame salt. Sesame and salt are slightly or well ground and combined into a condiment for use at table. Any kind of parched sesame may be used. It has a particularly important place in macrobiotics, no doubt because brown rice is scarcely edible without some salt at least.

gomoku meshi ごもくめし 五目飯 rice dish in which small pieces of chicken, tofu, and various vegetables in season are flavored with soy sauce and cooked with the rice. **Shiitake**, carrot, burdock, **konnyaku**, and **abura-age** are often used.

gomokuzushi ごもくずし 五目鮨 *See* Appendix 11.

gyokairui ぎょかいるい 魚介類 seafood; fish and shellfish.

gyokuro ぎょくろ 玉露 highest-quality green tea. *See also* Appendix 12.

gyoshō ぎょしょう 魚醬 *See* **uoshōyu**.

gyōza ギョーザ 餃子 a kind of Chinese dumpling (dim sum). A filling, usually of pork, cabbage, and **nira** minced to a fine paste, is used to fill circles of thin flour pastry shells with a scalloped join at the top. They are steam-fried or deep-fried or may be boiled in soup or **nabemono**. They are extremely popular and are often served at home as part of a regular Japanese meal.

gyūdon ぎゅうどん 牛丼 **donburi** dish featuring slices of beef.

gyū niku ぎゅうにく 牛肉 beef *Bos taurus*. After a long period in which the eating of beef was unthinkable, Emperor Meiji did his best to get the Japanese to eat beef, issuing a statement of approval in 1873. *Gyūnabe*, now called sukiyaki, had already appeared in the 1850s. **Shabu shabu** has also become a popular way of eating beef, as has **yakiniku**. Most of the Western ways of eating beef are also popular.

—H—

hachimitsu はちみつ 蜂蜜 honey. It is sometimes used to sweeten such things as **umeshu** but has little place in Japanese cuisine.

hadakamugi はだかむぎ 裸麦 naked barley, a variety of *Hordeum vulgare*. A species of barley particularly grown in western Japan. The grains closely resemble those of wheat.

hage はげ *See* **kawahagi**.

hajikami はじかみ 薑、椒 *See* **shōga**.

hakkō はっこう 発酵、醱酵 fermentation. The making of such products as saké, **shiokara**, and **nattō** involves a process of fermentation.

hakobe, hakobera はこべ、はこべら 繁縷 chickweed *Stellaria media*. *See also* **nanakusagayu**.

HAKUSAI

hakumai はくまい 白米 white (polished, or rather, milled) rice *Oryza sativa*. The short-grained subspecies *japonica* is the staple food of the Japanese. Milling reduces the grain to 90 to 92% of its unmilled size. The rice polishings (*nuka*) are used as a pickling base for a type of pickle called **nukazuke**. The normal cooking method is to steam-boil the rice in a tightly closed pot containing just the amount of water that will be absorbed by the time the rice is cooked. Automatic rice cookers remove all doubts and guesswork, the latest models being programmed with "neuro" and "fuzzy" chips, but they do not produce the crisp outer crust (*o-koge* 御焦げ), which is a great treat.

hakusai はくさい 白菜 Chinese cabbage *Brassica campestris* var. *amplexicaulis*. From autumn to spring, this large cabbage is used in all kinds of dishes, but especially in **nabemono** and **tsuke-mono**.

hama bōfu はまぼうふう 浜防風 *Glehnia littoralis*. A plant of the same family as **seri**, with a similar appearance except that it has red stems, it grows in the sands by the seashore. In spring the young shoots are eaten raw with sashimi and as a garnish for **sunomono** of fish. For summer use in **aemono** it is blanched both to remove the bitterness and to cook it.

hamachi はまち 魬 *See* **inada**.

hamaguri はまぐり 蛤、 文蛤、 蚌 Venus clam, hard clam *Meretrix lusoria*. These clams, about 8.5 cm long, 4 cm wide, and

HAMA BŌFŪ

6.5 cm high, gathered from the foreshores throughout Japan, are at their best from winter to spring. In the shell, they are served in **suimono**, barbecued, or steamed with saké. The flesh is used for sushi and clam rice and can be grilled on skewers.

hamo はも　鱧　pike conger *Muraenesox cinereus*. This sharp-toothed, 2-m-long eel comes mostly from the warm waters off central and western Japan, especially the Inland Sea. Its small bones are so prolific that a special knife (*hamokiri bōchō*) is used to bone it. At its best in summer, it is served as **kabayaki**, teriyaki, tempura, the special kind of pressed sushi called **oshizushi**, and **sunomono**.

hanami はなみ　花見　cherry-blossom viewing. Since ancient times the Japanese have taken great delight in the fleeting blossoms of the cherry tree. On Japan's four main islands, the trees bloom first in Kyushu, from the middle of March, and the blossoming follows the progress of spring, finally reaching the northernmost parts of the country in May. Parties are held day and night under the flowering trees, picnic foods are eaten, a lot of saké, beer, and other alcohol is drunk, and there is much singing, revelry, and enjoyment.

hanasakigani はなさきがに　花咲蟹　hanasaki crab, blue king crab *Paralithodes brevipes*. Similar to but smaller than the **tarabagani**, this delicious crab is prolific in the waters off the Nemuro Peninsula of northeastern Hokkaido. *See also* **kani**.

hangō はんごう 飯盒 outdoor rice cooker. A container, usually made of aluminum, in which sufficient rice for one or two people can be carried with the water necessary for cooking it. The rice and water are combined and the *hangō* is set over a fire until all the water is absorbed and the rice is ready.

hanpen はんぺん 半片 fish-paste cake. Whitefish such as shark is made into a paste with **yamanoimo**, spread into molds, and boiled till set. It can be eaten as it is with ginger-flavored soy sauce, but is most commonly served in **o-den**.

harusame はるさめ 春雨 "spring rain" noodles. The best quality, from China, are made from mung-bean starch. The Japanese ones are made from potato starch or sweet-potato starch. They are transparent, less than 1 mm thick, and from 20 to 30 cm long. As well as being used in **nabemono** and **sunomono**, they can be deep-fried, puffing up and becoming white.

hashi はし 箸 chopsticks. *See also* Appendix 1.

hassaku はっさく 八朔 hassaku orange *Citrus hassaku*. A very firm-fleshed, non-juicy, orange-type citrus fruit mostly grown in Wakayama, Ehime, and Hiroshima prefectures, where it originated. In season from December to April.

hasu はす 蓮、藕 lotus. *See also* **renkon**.

hasunomi はすのみ 蓮の実 lotus seed. In autumn these seeds can be eaten raw, having a mild sweetness, but usually they are preserved by boiling and drying. A paste made from lotus seeds is used as a filling for **wagashi**.

hata はた 羽太 grouper *Epinephelus septemfasciatus* (ma-hata). Reaching up to 90 cm in length, *ma-hata* is eaten from midsummer to early autumn as sashimi, **shioyaki**, and **nitsuke**. The much smaller *kijihata*, at around 40 cm, is particularly tasty.

hatahata はたはた 鰰、燭魚 sandfish *Arctoscopus japonicus*. A northern sea fish of about 15 to 25 cm in length, it is especially plentiful around Akita and Yamagata prefectures. It is a fairly fatty, white-fleshed fish and is eaten as tempura, sushi, **shioyaki**, and **nitsuke**. It is also dried, preserved as **shiokara**, and used as the basis for Akita's well-known **shottsuru**.

hatchō miso はっちょうみそ　八丁味噌　100% soybean miso. *See also* Appendix 6.

hatomugi はとむぎ　鳩麦　adlay *Coix lachryma-jobi* var. *ma-yuen*. A variety of Job's-tears, consumed for its nutritional qualities rather than its flavor, which is disappointing. Its flour can be mixed with wheat flour for whatever use, and the grains are parched, decocted, and made into a drink with boiling water.

hattai[ko] はったい[こ]　糗粉、麨粉　*See* **ōmugi**.

haze はぜ　沙魚、鯊　goby, gudgeon *Acanthogobius flavimanus* (ma-haze). The goby is widespread and exists in many species, but the well-known one of Tokyo Bay is the *ma-haze*, which grows to 20 cm or so. Its soft flesh is highly regarded and particularly good as tempura. For sashimi it is sliced into thin strips. It is also preserved as **kanroni**.

hechima へちま　糸瓜、天糸瓜　sponge gourd, loofah, luffa *Luffa cylindrica*. This plant grows in the south or Kyushu, and the young gourds are eaten in many ways, such as **sunomono** and **aemono**. It can also be briefly blanched and served with **sumiso**.

hie ひえ　稗　Japanese barnyard millet *Echinochloa utilis*. Formerly a staple of the Japanese diet, it is little eaten today. However, it is sometimes mixed with white rice, and can be made into **kayu** and **dango**.

higashi ひがし　干菓子　dry confectionary. One category of **wagashi**, *higashi* is any kind of dry candy such as toffee, and also includes **senbei**. In any case, the water content must be less than 20%. Most commonly, however, the word refers specifically to the little dry confections used in the tea ceremony. They are made from rice flour and sugar, which is colored and pressed into small, decorative molds. The best confections are made with **wasanbon**. Kyoto is particularly famous for its *higashi*.

hijiki ひじき 鹿尾菜、羊栖米 hijiki *Hizikia fusiforme*. A particularly nutritious seaweed that becomes a rich black when boiled before drying. *Hijiki mame* is an excellent and very popular dish, very rich in minerals and protein, in which soybeans and *hijiki*, both soaked, are sautéed in oil and seasoned with soy sauce and sugar.

hikiniku ひきにく 挽き肉 ground meat, minced meat, mince. Japanese butchers normally sell a variety of minced meats such as beef, pork, and chicken. Minced meat is used in **tsukune**, **soboro**, **gyōza**, and the cabbage rolls that are often found in **o-den**.

himono ひもの 干物 dried fish. Sun, wind, and dry night air are all used to dry a variety of lightly salted fish. Before drying they can be grilled or seasoned with **mirin**. The best way to eat them is hot from the grill.

hina matsuri ひなまつり 雛祭 festival for girls held on March 3. Also called the doll festival because of the display of dolls set up in houses where there is a girl. Traditional foods include diamond-shaped rice cakes called *hishimochi* colored white, pink, and green, as well as *shirozake*, a white-colored drink made from glutinous rice, rice mold, and **mirin**.

hirame ひらめ 平目、鮃、比目魚 bastard halibut, false halibut *Paralichthys olivaceus*. At its best from September to February, this is a highly regarded fish that can be prepared in every way. Since it sometimes harbors nematode parasites, it is safer cooked rather than eaten as sashimi or sushi.

hiratake ひらたけ 平茸 oyster mushroom *Pleurotus ostreatus*. This mushroom, gray-capped and white-fleshed, 5 to 15 cm across the cap, is delicious when gathered from the wild from spring till autumn. The less delicious cultivated version is usually marketed under the name of **shimeji**.

hiroshima na ひろしまな 広島菜 a variety of *Brassica campestris* var. *chinensis*. This green-leaved vegetable is cultivated almost exclusively for making Hiroshima's famous salt pickle.

hishinomi ひしのみ 菱の実 water chestnut, water caltrop *Trapa bispinosa* var. *iinumai*. Young ones are eaten raw; harder, more mature ones are boiled, grilled, and then eaten. They are rather like chestnuts to eat but are not used in cooking.

hishio ひしお 醤 Historically *hishio* has a very important place in Japan's food culture. There were originally three types: 草醤 *kusa bishio*, equivalent to today's **tsukemono**; 肉醤 *shishi bishio*, equivalent to **shiokara**; and 穀醤 *koku bishio*, fermented grain products such as miso and soy sauce. It is from the latter that modern *hishio*, popular in western Japan, has developed. Vegetables such as eggplant, ginger, and **shirouri**, with hulled, split soybeans, are fermented in a kind of barley miso. It is a high-class product of limited availability. *See also* **morokyū**.

hiyamugi ひやむぎ 冷麦 dried noodle made of wheat, in thickness coming between **sōmen** and **udon**. After boiling, the noodles are chilled and served with a fairly chili-hot dipping broth. A summer dish.

hiyashi ひやし… 冷し… cold. Generally prefixed to the names of foods normally expected to be hot, e.g., *hiyashi sōmen*.

hiyayakko ひややっこ 冷奴 cold tofu. A simple dish in which a block of cold tofu is eaten with finely sliced welsh onion, grated ginger, **kezuribushi**, and soy sauce.

hōbō ほうぼう 魴鮄、竹麦魚 bluefin gurnard, bluefin sea-robin *Chelidonichthys spinosus*. A highly regarded, white-fleshed fish about 40 cm long, at its best in winter. It is used in soups and **nabemono** and is also good as **shioyaki** and **agemono**.

hōchō ほうちょう 包丁 Japanese cook's knife. Apart from the fact that they cut, these knives are in a different world from anything known in Western culture. Like swords, they are forged and are sharpened on one side of the blade only, allowing extremely clean, accurate slicing. They must be sharpened on several different whetstones, a knife steel being totally unsuitable. The three main types are *sashimi bōchō*; *deba bōchō*, for dealing with fish, apart from sashimi; and *usuba bōchō*, for fine work with vegetables. A good cutler might sell over fifty different kinds of knives made from traditionally forged steel.

hōjicha ほうじちゃ　培じ茶　parched **bancha**. *See also* **cha** and Appendix 12.

hojiso ほじそ　穂紫蘇　stem (spike) of young budding **shiso**. The little buds are scraped off to be used as a condiment. Pickled *hojiso* is served with **shiruko**.

hokkai ebi ほっかいえび　北海海老　Hokkai shrimp *Pandalus kessleri*. About 13 cm long, this shrimp is prolific off the northern shores of Hokkaido. It can be prepared as **tsukudani**, though much of the catch is peeled and canned.

hokke ほっけ　𩸽　Atka mackerel *Pleurogrammus azonus*. Caught in large quantity in the northern waters from the beginning of winter to the following spring, this fish is about 40 cm long. Very good when quite fresh, it does not keep well because of its high fat content. It is usually grilled or simmered as **nimono**.

hokki gai ほっきがい　北寄貝　surf clam, hen clam *Spisula sachalinensis*. This clam, which is also called *ubagai*, is about 9.5 cm long, 4.5 cm wide, and 7.5 cm high and is most prolific in the Sanriku and Hokkaido areas. The flesh has an off-white color but turns pink when boiled. At its best from spring to summer, it is served as sashimi, sushi, **yakimono**, **sunomono**, and in **suimono**.

hone nuki ほねぬき　骨抜き　tweezers for removing fish bones.

honshimeji ほんしめじ　本湿地　honshimeji *Lyophyllum shimeji*. An autumn mushroom of excellent flavor, it is difficult to cultivate and what is widely sold as (cultivated) *honshimeji* is actually *buna shimeji* (*Hypsizigus marmoreus*). **Shimeji** is used in soups, tempura, and **nitsuke**. According to one saying, **matsutake** is for aroma, *shimeji* for flavor.

honzen ryōri ほんぜんりょうり　本膳料理　The *zen* of the name refers to the short-legged trays on which this formal style of food is served. It is one of the three basic styles of traditional cooking, the other two being **kaiseki ryōri 1** and **2**, both of which are at present more frequently served than *honzen ryōri*. The menu has a highly formalized structure based on **ichijū sansai**, which can be extended to two soups and five or seven side dishes, or three soups and eleven side dishes, which should emphasize variety of flavor. This formal style of cooking is for the most part found only at weddings and funerals.

horagai ほらがい　法螺貝、 吹螺、 梭尾螺　trumpet shell *Charonia tritonis*. The flesh from this large shell, up to 40 cm long and 19 cm in diameter, is eaten raw as sashimi, **sunomono**, and **aemono**. It is also baked in the shell as **tsuboyaki**.

hōrensō ほうれんそう　法蓮草、菠薐草　spinach *Spinacia oleracea*. A favorite vegetable in Japan, it is a frequent ingredient of soups, but is at its best in the cooked salad *hōrensō no goma ae*. It also makes excellent **o-hitashi**.

hōroku ほうろく　焙烙　round earthenware platter. Used for parching seeds and grains as well as tea and salt, it usually has a domed lid so that it can be used for steam-baking (*hōroku-yaki*). In this style of cooking, the ingredients are usually set on a bed of pine needles and are cooked and served in the *hōroku*.

horumon ryōri ホルモンりょうり　ホルモン料理　offal, variety meats. This kind of cooking originated among Korean residents of Japan. The name "hormone" derives from the fact that many of these organs are glands. Pork, beef, and chicken organs are used. They are either grilled as **yakiniku** or **yakitori**, or are used in the one-pot dish called *motsunabe*. As well as heart, liver, and gizzard, tripe is extensively used.

hotategai ほたてがい　帆立貝　scallop *Patinopecten yessoensis*. A large bivalve, up to 20 cm across, it is prolific in the waters of northern Honshu and Hokkaido and is extensively farmed. It is especially prized for its tender adductor muscle (**kaibashira**), which makes delicious sashimi. In cooking, the female (red) roe

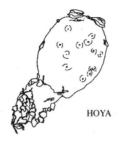

HOYA

and male (cream) roe, and often the mantle, are usually left attached to the muscle. Scallops are served in soups, **nimono**, **yakimono**, and **agemono**.

hotokenoza ほとけのざ　仏の座　henbit *Lamium amplexicaule*. *See also* **nanakusagayu**.

hoya ほや　海鞘、老海鼠　sea squirt Class Ascidiacea, especially *doroboya* (*Corella japonica*) and *eboya* (*Styela clava*). Somewhat limited in appeal, these creatures are present in all the waters surrounding Japan, but are particularly prolific in the coastal areas of Sanriku and north of Akita. Their best season is July and August. They are eaten raw after being skinned and their intestines are served in **sunomono**. Fermented sea-squirt intestines are a kind of **shiokara** similar to **konowata**.

—I—

ichigo いちご　苺　strawberry *Fragaria x ananassa*. A very popular fruit frequently served with condensed milk rather than cream at the end of a meal. Strawberry jam is also very popular. The winter availability of empty rice fields and the unsuitability of Japan's humid rainy season and hot summer have led to the practice of growing strawberries in vinyl houses on the empty fields in winter and spring. Donner, *harunoka*, *toyonoka*, *fukuba*, *nyohō*, and *hōkōwase* are widely grown varieties.

ICHIMONJI

ichijiku イチジク　無花果、映日果　fig *Ficus carica*. Introduced into Japan in the early seventeenth century, the fig has a restricted place among the autumn dessert fruits.

ichijū sansai いちじゅうさんさい　一汁三菜　one soup, three vegetables. This combination is the basis on which Japanese menus are constructed. Apart from rice, there should be soup and at least three dishes containing vegetables, customarily from the categories of **namasu**, **nimono**, and **yakimono**.

ichimi tōgarashi いちみとうがらし　一味唐辛子　ground chili pepper. *See also* **shichimi tōgarashi**.

ichimonji いちもんじ　一文字　scraper-spatula. The handle of this utensil is vertical to the blade, which makes it particularly useful in cooking **o-konomiyaki**.

ichiyazuke いちやづけ　一夜漬け　*See* **tsukemono**.

igai いがい　貽貝　mussel *Mytilus coruscus*. As often as not, mussels are called *mūrugai* ムール貝, from the French *moule*, meaning mussel. At their best when steam-baked as *hōroku-yaki*, they are also good boiled, baked, and as **sunomono**. Their season is from January to March. A similar but rather larger mussel is the **karasugai**, which, though edible, has a muddy smell. In some parts of Japan *igai* is called *karasugai*.

iidako いいだこ　飯蛸　*See* **tako**.

ika いか　烏賊　squid: various dibranchiate cephalopods. Squid are a popular everyday food throughout Japan. They can be anything from bite-size to 50 cm long and are a cheap source of good protein, very low in fat. Above all served as sushi and sashimi, squid is also served as tempura and grilled, especially as teriyaki. Dried squid (**surume**) is a favorite snack with drinks.

ikanago いかなご 玉筋魚 Pacific sandlance *Ammodytes personatus*. Best when it is five to six months old and about 10 cm long. It is boiled in salt water and cooled, then served in vinegar-flavored soy sauce or **sumiso**. It is also made into tempura, **tsukudani**, and dried.

ikanago shōyu いかなごしょうゆ 玉筋魚醤油 *See* **uoshōyu**.

ikizukuri いきづくり 生き作り、活き造り *See* **sashimi**.

ikura イクラ salmon eggs. Though hardly to be compared with caviar, these shiny red eggs are considered a luxury and are very good as a topping for sushi. The word *ikura* is derived from the Russian word *ikra*, meaning fish eggs. For salmon roe in the piece, *see also* **sujiko**.

imo いも 芋、藷、薯 potato. Japan has a wide range of potatoes, including yams, sweet potato, and taro. *See also* **jagaimo**, **yamanoimo**, **satsumaimo**, and **satoimo**.

inada いなだ 鰤 yellowtail, Japanese amberjack *Seriola quinqueradiata*. Called **hamachi** in western Japan and increasingly so in other parts of the country, this is the young of **buri**, about 40 cm long. It is preferable to *buri* for sushi and sashimi and is very good grilled as **shioyaki**. Best in summer.

inarizushi いなりずし 稲荷鮨 *See* Appendix 11.

ingenmame いんげんまめ 隠元豆 kidney bean *Phaseolus vulgaris*. The mature beans are mostly dried and then prepared as **nimono**, **an**, or *amanattō*, a kind of **wagashi**. For the young bean, *see also* **sayaingen**.

inobuta いのぶた 猪豚 boar-pig cross. The flesh of this creature has the best of both worlds: the tenderness of pork and the lean gaminess of wild boar. It makes an excellent **nabemono**.

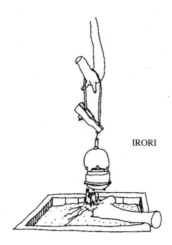

IRORI

inoshishi いのしし 猪 wild boar *Sus scrofa*. Boars are still reasonably prevalent in Honshu, Shikoku, and Kyushu. The best wild boar comes from the young animals in winter. Wild boar is also referred to as *yama kujira* (mountain whale) and *botan* (peony) and is not always wild. *See also* **botan nabe**.

ippin ryōri いっぴんりょうり 一品料理 a la carte. On a menu, this most frequently indicates dishes ordered separately to be eaten with drinks.

irigoma いりごま 煎り胡麻、炒り胡麻 parched sesame. Sesame seeds are normally parched before use, a task that requires skill and attention to avoid overcooking.

iriko いりこ 煎り子、炒り子 small dried fish used for making **dashi**.

irori いろり 囲炉裏、炉 central hearth. The hearth was formerly a feature of Japanese houses in mountainous areas, and many still exist, especially in country restaurants, for nostalgic effect. Part of the dining-kitchen area of a house, the hearth was adjacent to the *doma*, the beaten-earth floor area for food preparation at the lower, ground level. Although some cooking was done at the *irori*, its main purposes were heating and drying. *See also* **o-yaki**, **kiri-tanpo**, and Appendix 3.

isaki いさき　伊佐木、伊佐幾　grunt *Parapristipoma trilineatum*.
Found in the warmer western waters, this fish grows up to 40 cm
in length. Best in summer, it makes good sashimi when very fresh.
Otherwise, it is cooked as **shioyaki** or **furai**.

ise ebi いせえび　伊勢海老　crawfish, Japanese spiny lobster *Pan-
ulirus japonicus*. This crustacean can reach 35 cm, though is usually smaller, not least because the Japanese waters are becoming
seriously depleted. It makes excellent but rather expensive sashimi, and is very good split in half and grilled.

ishikarinabe いしかりなべ　石狩鍋　salmon hodgepodge. A famous
nabemono of Hokkaido. Salmon, with both hard and soft roe, is
cooked in a large pot of **dashi** with miso and various vegetables,
tofu, and **konnyaku**. The diner adds a sprinkling of **sanshō** powder at the time of eating.

ishiyaki いしやき　石焼き　baking on hot stones, in one of two
different contexts. In the first, chestnuts and sweet potatoes are
cooked in hot pebbles by street vendors, often itinerant. The second setting is a high-class restaurant (**ryōtei**), where a hot stone,
slices of abalone (and other things), and a dipping sauce are placed
in front of the diner. The food is cooked on the stone, dipped, and
eaten immediately.

ishiyaki imo いしやきいも　石焼き芋　baked sweet potato. Itinerant vendors bake sweet potatoes in hot pebbles and sell them at all
hours of day and night. They are very popular with children after
school and adults returning home late from work or drinking. The
vendor is announced by a steam whistle or traditional cry.

isobe いそべ　磯辺　prefix for dishes prepared or garnished with
nori. A typical example is *hōrensō no isobemaki*, in which spinach
leaves that have been lightly boiled are served rolled up in **nori**.

itadori いたどり　虎杖　Japanese knotweed, flowering bamboo
Polygonum cuspidatum. Found in the mountains in spring, when
the shoots are 20 to 25 cm long. The shoots are peeled and eaten

raw with salt, and have a slightly acidic taste. *Itadori* is also used in **nimono**. *See also* **sansai**, **sansai ryōri**, and Appendix 9.

itamae いたまえ 板前 chef (for Japanese cooking). Whereas **chōrishi** refers to qualifications, *itamae* refers to the cook's position at the head of the kitchen team. The word *itamae* literally means in front of the chopping board.

itamemono いためもの 炒め物 shallow-fried dish. The Japanese equivalent of Chinese stir-frying. A flat-bottomed frying pan is used with very little oil.

itawasa いたわさ 板山葵 sliced **kamaboko** served with **wasabi** and soy sauce.

itayagai いたやがい 板屋貝 bay scallop *Pecten albicans* (syn. *Pecten laquetus*). Similar in all important respects to **hotategai** only much smaller (up to 12 cm across). Found along all the coasts of Japan except northern Hokkaido. *Itayagai* is more or less the same as the St. James shell, coquille Saint-Jacques (*Pecten jacobaeus*). *See also* **hotategai** for culinary uses.

iwana いわな 岩魚 char *Salvelinus leucomaenis*. Lives in cold mountain streams and grows to a length of about 30 cm. At its best from May until summer, it is cooked in the same ways as other trout. *See also* **kawamasu**.

iwanori いわのり 岩海苔 *See* **nori**.

iwashi いわし 鰯、鰮 sardine, pilchard *Sardinops melanostictus* (ma-iwashi). An abundant fish in quantity, species, and local names, the smaller ones (less than 10 cm) are at their best in June, whereas the larger ones are better from August to October. They make very good, cheap sashimi, and in some places itinerant street vendors fillet them in front of customers' houses. They can be made into tempura and **dango** and have many other uses.

iwatake いわたけ 岩茸、石茸 *Umbilicaria esculenta*. A lichen that is collected at great danger from cliff faces, it is considered a great and rather expensive delicacy. *Iwatake* lives on the cliff

JINGISUKAN NABE

faces for a century or more and is gathered by rappelling (abseiling) collectors. It is thoroughly washed to remove the dust that has collected over the years, soaked for two days, then made into tempura or **sunomono**. It is mostly harvested in Shikoku, but formerly in many other parts of Japan as well. Very limited in appeal, it is nevertheless considered a great luxury, probably for reasons other than its flavor.

iyokan いよかん　伊予柑 Iyo orange *Citrus iyo*. Although this delicious orange is named after a former province in Shikoku, it was developed in Yamaguchi in 1886. As well as being eaten fresh, it is much used in marmalade making.

izakaya いざかや　居酒屋 simple tavern, where customers eat and drink at small expense in a cheerful atmosphere.

—J—

jagaimo じゃがいも　じゃが芋 potato *Solanum tuberosum*. Many varieties are grown in Japan, one of the most popular being May Queen メークイーン. The potato is particularly associated with Hokkaido, where it is grown extensively. It goes well in **nimono**, **o-den**, and soups, and is much used in Western-style cooking. Potato starch has many uses, having all but replaced true **katakuriko**. Potato is also called **bareisho** 馬鈴薯.

JUNSAI

jinenjo じねんじょ　自然薯　*See* **yamanoimo**.

jingisukan nabe ジンギスカンなべ　成吉思汗鍋　Genghis Khan hot plate. For this dish, which comes from Mongolia, mutton and vegetables are cooked on a domed, shield-shaped hot plate, which is ribbed and often has holes in it. The grilled food is dipped in a sauce strongly flavored with garlic and eaten. It is a kind of **yakiniku**.

jizake じざけ　地酒　local saké. A saké of small production, for the most part drunk where it is produced. Many such sakés are excellent and are sometimes available beyond their locality or can be obtained by delivery service.

jōshinko じょうしんこ　上糝粉　*See* **shinko 2**.

jūbako じゅうばこ　重箱　tiered food box. Usually in three layers, these boxes are lacquered and can be great works of art. They are used at New Year and other festive times to house special foods. *See also* **jūzume** and **o-sechi ryōri**.

junsai じゅんさい　蓴菜　water shield *Brasenia schreberi*. A little water plant growing in ponds and marshes that has long, thread-like stems thrown up from the root. In spring and early summer these produce leafy shoots enclosed in a gelatinous sheath, which float on the surface and are gathered from small boats. It is an expensive delicacy with virtually no flavor, appreciated for its gelatinous texture. Often served in **suimono**, it is almost impossible to retrieve with chopsticks. It is also prepared as **aemono** and is eaten with soy sauce and **wasabi**, and also with **sanbaizu**. It is sold loose (in plastic bags) and in bottles.

jūzume じゅうづめ 重詰め food arranged in a **jūbako**. The box can have up to five tiers, and there are traditional rules for arranging the food.

—K—

kabayaki かばやき 蒲焼 one kind of **yakimono**, in which the fish is opened up, boned, and skewered, then grilled while being basted with a thick, sweet sauce. Eel *kabayaki* (*unaginokabayaki*) is justifiably the best-known dish of this kind. Served on a bowl of hot rice, it is one of Japan's great treats.

kabocha かぼちゃ 南瓜 pumpkin, winter squash *Cucurbita moschata*. The Japanese pumpkin, though fairly small, makes very good tempura and is also served as **aemono**. When simmered as **nimono** or steamed as **mushimono**, the skin becomes tender enough to eat. *Kikuza* and *bizen chirimen* are popular varieties.

kabosu かぼす *Citrus sphaerocarpa*. A juicy, green citrus fruit with the sharpness of lemon, it is used instead of vinegar to make **sunomono** and **ponzu** for **nabemono**. Its largest crop is in September and October.

kabu かぶ 蕪、蕪菁 turnip *Brassica campestris* var. *glabra*. One of Japan's old vegetables, formerly called **suzuna**. Harvested in autumn and winter, it comes in all sizes and several colors. Red *akakabu* should not be confused with beetroot, since they are only superficially similar. *Kabu* and *maru daikon* (large spherical white radish) are also easily confused. The famous Kyoto pickle **senmaizuke** is made from the particularly large *shōgoin kabu*. Mostly the root of *kabu* is eaten, but some turnips are grown for their leaves. Japanese turnips are tenderer than Western ones, and very white. There are many good recipes for *kabu*, and many **tsukemono** are made from turnips. *Kabu* is also known as *kabura* かぶら 蕪、蕪菁.

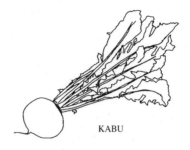

KABU

kagami mochi かがみもち　鏡餅　big fat round rice cake in the traditional shape of a mirror (*kagami*). Two or three of these cakes, of different sizes, one on top of the other, form the basis of the New Year decoration in homes. They are decorated with **daidai**, **konbu**, dried persimmons, and other traditional items. On January 11 the cakes are usually cut up and served in **zōni** or **shiruko**.

kai かい　貝　(properly *kairui* かいるい　貝類) mollusk. The expression literally means shell, but since *kai* does not include prawns, crabs, and lobsters, shellfish is not a satisfactory translation. All kinds of mollusks are great favorites in Japan.

kaibashira かいばしら　貝柱　adductor muscle of bivalve shellfish. The best-known *kaibashira* is that of the scallop, which is quite large. That of **tairagi** is also large, but those of **bakagai**, which has two, are somewhat smaller. They are all versatile, being eaten as sashimi, sushi, tempura, **sunomono**, **suimono**, and **nabemono**.

kaiseki ryōri 1. かいせきりょうり　会席料理　The two kinds of *kaiseki* have different purposes. This one is for drinking alcohol, whereas **2** is for drinking tea and is frequently called **cha kaiseki**. Drinking is not conducive to formality and *kaiseki ryōri 1*, served in a context of singing, clapping, entertainment, revelry, and camaraderie, does not have a formal basis such as **honzen ryōri**. The simple basis of **ichijū sansai** is supplemented with a series of dishes to go with drinks (**sakana 1**), including such things as sashimi, tempura, **aemono**, and **sunomono**. When the drinking

KAKI

has stopped, rice, **miso shiru**, and pickles are served to conclude the party.

kaiseki ryōri 2. かいせきりょうり　懐石料理　This kind of meal was developed to accompany the tea ceremony, for which *see also* **cha kaiseki** and Appendix 13. *Cha kaiseki* is characterized by formality and restraint, great emphasis being placed on the seasonality of the food and the suitability and beauty of the vessels.

kaisō かいそう　海藻　seaweed. Many different kinds of seaweed, especially **nori** and **konbu**, are eaten, forming an important part of the Japanese diet.

kaiware かいわれ　貝割　young shoots (cotyledon) of **daikon** and **kabu**. They are extensively used as a salad and garnish, of sushi in particular.

kajiki かじき　梶木、　旗魚　marlin, swordfish *Tetrapturus audax* (ma-kajiki). The marlins are large fishes. *Ma-kajiki* grows up to 3 m long and 100 kg in weight. Others are bigger and smaller. In all cases their flesh is like tuna and they are eaten as sashimi.

kaki 1. かき　牡蠣　oyster *Crassostrea gigas*. Many places in Japan are famous for their oysters, which were first cultivated in Hiroshima in A.D. 1673. They are now cultivated on a very large scale, and as well as being eaten raw, they are served as **sugaki**, **furai**, **nabemono**, and cooked with rice (*kakimeshi*). Shoopers should be aware of the distinction between oysters for cooking and those for eating raw, especially since oysters are the cause of a lot of hepatitis. Vinegar masks the smell of raw oysters but does not

KAMABOKO

remove the danger of contracting hepatitis from oysters grown in polluted waters.

kaki 2. かき 柿 Japanese persimmon *Diospyros kaki*. A very popular autumn fruit eaten raw and also made into a very attractive confection dried. Although many of the Japanese varieties of persimmon are sweet (*amagaki*) and can be eaten raw straight from the tree, many other varieties (*shibugaki*) have an astringency that must be removed before the fruit can be eaten. *Fuyū gaki* is a well-known sweet variety, and *Saijō*, astringent. Dried persimmons form part of the New Year decoration.

kakiage かきあげ 掻き揚げ one kind of tempura. Small fish, shellfish, and shrimps are made into tempura as a clump. Vegetables such as carrot, burdock, and onion are also chopped small and prepared in the same way.

kama かま 釜 rice-cooking pot. A large, deep pot with a flange around the circumference to support it in the hole on top of the **kamado**. It has a heavy wooden lid with two crosspieces on it to prevent steam from escaping during cooking. It has largely been displaced by the automatic rice cooker.

kamaboko かまぼこ 蒲鉾 fish-paste loaf. The flesh of many different kinds of fish both white and dark can be used, but probably shark is most common. A paste (**surimi**) is made, thickened with starch, sometimes colored pink and green, molded into pillows on a little board, and steamed. It is sliced to serve and may be eaten as is with soy sauce at breakfast or as **tsumamimono**. It can also be added to **o-den**. *Yakikamaboko* (commercially grilled) is also very good, as is **agekamaboko**.

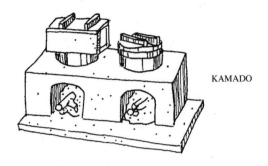

KAMADO

kamado かまど 竈 kitchen range, also called *kudo* and *hettsui*. This was built on the beaten earth floor (*doma*) of the traditional kitchen, but nowadays usually on a concrete floor. The *kamado* is a kind of enclosed fireplace for a wood fire, with openings in the top for rice-cooking pots (**kama**) and the pans used for making **miso shiru**. Each pot has its own fire. The *kamado* is not used for other cooking, though sometimes a facility for heating water is incorporated, and occasionally it is used in the domestic manufacture of miso. Traditionally there was no flue.

kama meshi かまめし 釜飯 prepared in individual **kama**, this is a dish of rice cooked with other ingredients, created in the late nineteenth century in Asakusa, Tokyo. Prawns, oysters, scallops, and salmon are used, as well as **shiitake** mushrooms, bamboo shoots, and chicken. It is sometimes sold as **ekiben**.

kamasu かます 魳、 梭魚 barracuda, sea pike *Sphyraena japonica*. Not one of the best eating fish, it is rather watery and is best as **shioyaki**, **kara-age**, or **furai**. *Akakamasu*, one of the better barracudas, is at its best in summer. It grows to a length of 40 to 50 cm. Some barracudas are poisonous.

kamo かも 鴨 wild duck *Anas platyrhynchos*. True wild duck is not often available and *kamo* can be a euphemism for *ahiru*, domestic duck, or an abbreviation for *aigamo*, which is what is normally eaten. *Aigamo*, a cross between wild and domestic duck, is not a game bird, whereas *kamo* is. Both are used in soups and sukiyaki and grilled and steamed.

kanbutsu かんぶつ 乾物 dried food. A general term for all dried food, though dried fish are called **himono**.

kani かに 蟹 crab. One of the food delights of winter, of which there are many kinds. *See also* **hanasakigani**, **kegani**, **matsubagani**, **sawagani**, **tarabagani**, **watarigani**, and **zuwaigani**.

kani miso かにみそ 蟹味噌 brown cream inside a crab shell. Consisting mostly of the reproductive organs, it is considered a great delicacy (**chinmi**). It can either be eaten as is straight from the shell of a boiled crab, or further cooked after seasoning with saké, sugar, and egg yolk.

kanmi かんみ 甘味 sweetness. The technical word for sweetness as one of the five basic tastes in the Far East: salty, sour, bitter, sweet, and (in China) pepper hot and (in Japan) tasty. *See also* Appendix 14.

kanmidokoro かんみどころ 甘味処 traditional teashop. Traditional dessert-like sweets such as **mitsumame** are served with green tea.

kanpyō かんぴょう 干瓢、乾瓢 dried gourd strip. *Kanpyō* is the cream-colored flesh of the white-flowered gourd **yūgao**, cut into very long thin strips and dried. Its best-known use is as part of the filling for **makizushi**, but it is also used in soups, **aemono**, and as an edible tie or string. In **shōjin ryōri** it is sometimes used to make vegetarian stock. In damp weather it easily goes moldy.

kanroni かんろに 甘露煮 1. a kind of **nimono** in which various small fish such as **ayu**, **funa**, and **haze** are simmered very slowly in a mixture of soy sauce, **mirin**, and syrup until they are dry and glistening. 2. the candying of chestnuts, kumquats, and other fruit in unflavored syrup.

kanrozuke かんろづけ 甘露漬け 1. candied preserves. Green Japanese apricots (*aoume*) and the peel of various citrus fruits

such as **zabon** are candied with sugar. 2. in northern Japan a preserve of **kazunoko** that is made with soy sauce, saké, and **kōji**, to
be eaten at New Year.

kanten かんてん 寒天 agar-agar *Gelidium amansii*. A jelly-like
substance made from the red alga **tengusa**. *Kanten* is eaten with
vinegar and soy sauce and is used like gelatin to make jellied dishes. However, it melts at a higher temperature than gelatin, and is
therefore more useful in hot weather.

kappa かっぱ 河童 sushi-shop word for cucumber. Lightly pickled cucumber wrapped up in **nori** seaweed with sushi rice is called
kappamaki. *Kappa* is a mythical monkey-like mischievous creature that lives in ponds and rivers and likes to eat the cucumbers
thrown to pacify it.

kappō かっぽう 割烹 1. high-class cookery. 2. high-class Japanese-style restaurant.

kara-age からあげ 唐揚げ、空揚げ one method of deep-frying.
The ingredients are either deep-fried as they are, or more usually dusted with seasoned flour and deep-fried. *Kara-age* of both
chicken and flounder is popular, but vegetables can also be done.

karafuto masu からふとます 樺太鱒 pink salmon *Oncorhynchus
gorbuscha*. This salmon, about 50 cm in length, is mostly canned.
It is also a good source of **ikura** and **sujiko**.

karashi からし 芥子、辛子 mustard *Brassica nigra*; *Sinapis alba*;
Brassica juncea. Japanese mustard is even hotter than English
mustard. This is because it is simply a blend of the ground seeds
of different mustards without the addition of flour. Mixing with
hot water (40°C) and waiting a few minutes brings out the heat. It
serves as a condiment for **o-den** and is used to make **tsukemono**
and dressings.

karashi sumiso からしすみそ 芥子酢味噌、辛子酢味噌 white
miso flavored with mustard and vinegar. Used as a dressing for
aemono, especially of fish, it is particularly good with the **konnyaku** slices called **yama fugu**.

karasugai からすがい 烏貝 *See* **igai**.

karasumi からすみ 鱲子 botargo (dried, salted mullet roe). This is one of the three superlative delicacies (*tenka no sandai chinmi* 天下の三大珍味), the other two being **konowata** and **uni**. The dried roe is eaten as it is, thinly sliced, but may be lightly grilled.

karei かれい 鰈 flatfish, flounder. The eyes on the right (dextral flatfish) are said to distinguish *karei* from **hirame**, which has the eyes on the left (sinistral flatfish). The distinction is not valid, however, for there are right-eye *karei* like *ma-garei*, Family Pleuronectidae, and left-eye *karei* like *yarigarei*, Family Bothidae. Either way, they are delicious, especially as sashimi, **yakimono**, and **agemono**. At Onomichi in Hiroshima Prefecture small ones are dried and called *debira*.

karē ko カレーこ カレー粉 curry powder. It was introduced to Japan from England in the latter part of the nineteenth century and is mostly used for making English-style curry. However, it is sometimes used to flavor the soup for **udon** and **soba**.

karin かりん 花梨、 榠樝 Chinese quince *Chaenomeles sinensis*. The Chinese quince is similar in shape and color to the roughly ovoid Western quince (**marumero**). However, it has an astringency that must be removed by boiling before use in other ways. An autumn fruit, it is mostly candied or made into jams and jellies.

karintō かりんとう 花林糖 one kind of candy (*kakemono-gashi*). Pieces of paste made from flour, water, and egg are thoroughly deep-fried and then coated with sugar, usually brown. This candy is said to date from the Heian period (794–1185).

kashi かし 菓子 sweetmeat, confection, "cake." *See also* **wagashi**.

kashiwa かしわ commonly used as a word for chicken meat, strictly speaking, *kashiwa* refers to the chicken wing. It is considered to have a particularly rich flavor and is very good deep-fried.

kashiwa mochi かしわもち 柏餅 round-shaped **mochi** filled with **an** and wrapped in an oak leaf. It is especially eaten on May 5,

Children's Day (formerly Boys' Day), the symbolism being that oak leaves do not wither.

kasu かす　粕、糟　saké lees. *See also* **sakekasu**.

kasutera カステラ　Castella cake. This sponge cake, made of flour, eggs, and sugar, was introduced to Japan by the Portuguese in the sixteenth century. The improvised oven, necessary because the Japanese did not have ovens, gives the cake the texture of a steamed cake. Usually very sweet, it is made by specialist bakers and is often given as a gift.

katakuchi iwashi　かたくちいわし　片口鰯　anchovy *Engraulis japonicus*. This large-mouthed fish grows to a length of 15 cm and is best from September to February. The best way to eat it is raw, straight out of the water, with a dressing of **sumiso** or ginger-flavored soy sauce. Most of the catch is preserved in various ways, especially by drying.

katakuriko　かたくりこ　片栗粉　1. flour of Japanese dog's tooth violet *Erythronium japonicum*. This thickening starch is now so expensive that it is used only for top-quality cookery and confectionary. 2. Under the same name, potato starch is now normally used as a cheap substitute.

katsu　カツ　a kind of **agemono** of meat, fish, or chicken coated with egg and bread crumbs and deep-fried. The word *katsu* comes from cutlet, presumably because lamb, veal, and pork cutlets are often cooked in this way. The English word has no reference at all to the method of cooking, being the name of a cut of meat.

katsudon　カツどん　カツ丼　pork **donburi** dish. Rice is placed in a large bowl and a slice of pork, fried in egg and bread crumbs, is set on top with onion and sweet stock. A lightly mixed egg is poured over and cooked by the heat of the rice and meat. The dish was thought up by a high school boy in 1923 and today is very popular.

katsuo　かつお　鰹　skipjack, oceanic bonito *Katsuwonus pelamis*. Although this fish reaches a length of 1 m and a weight of between 18 and 25 kg, those caught in the waters off Japan are mostly half

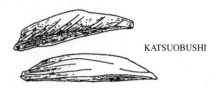

KATSUOBUSHI

that size. They are fished in early summer off southeastern Hokkaido and in autumn in the warmer waters off southern Japan. They are good as teriyaki and sashimi, especially **tataki**, but a large part of the catch goes into the manufacture of **katsuobushi**.

katsuobushi かつおぶし　鰹節　dried, smoked, mold-cured bonito. The filleted fish is boiled, dried, smoked, and cured with the mold *Aspergillus glaucus*. When the fillets are as hard as a piece of wood, they are shaved, and it is the shavings that have numerous uses. Above all, they are used to make soup stock, but are also extensively used as a flavoring and a garnish for such dishes as cold tofu and **aemono**. *See also* Appendix 2.

katsuobushibako　かつおぶしばこ　鰹節箱　box for shaving **katsuobushi**. A wood plane is mounted upside down on top of a box to receive the shavings, which collect in a drawer. Using this box was once a normal domestic accomplishment, but nowadays its use is largely restricted to professionals in high-class establishments.

kawahagi かわはぎ　皮剥　leatherjacket, filefish, threadsail fish *Stephanolepis cirrhifer*. In western Japan known as *hage*, this is an excellent eating fish that can grow to 30 cm long but is usually taken smaller. At its best in summer, it is very good prepared as **nitsuke**, the liver particularly so. It is also eaten as sashimi and **furai**.

kawamasu かわます　川鱒、河鱒　brook trout, brook char *Salvelinus fontinalis*. Introduced from North America, this trout is from 20 to 50 cm long and flourishes in the cool river waters of northern Japan. It is at its best from late September to December and is good sautéed or cooked as **shioyaki** of **furai**.

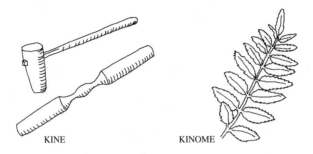

KINE   KINOME

kawano natsudaidai かわのなつだいだい 川野夏橙 *See* **ama-natsu**.

kayu かゆ 粥 rice porridge. Usually given the honorific *o-*,i.e., *o-kayu*, this is primarily a breakfast dish. In the classic version, rice is cooked in much more water than usual and salt and sometimes other things are included. The simplest addition is **umeboshi**, but salmon, salmon roe, and cod roe are good, with **mitsuba**, **seri**, **yuzu**, **kinome**, or **sanshō** as flavoring.

kazunoko かずのこ 数の子、鯟 prepared herring roe. It may be either salted or dried, but nowadays most *kazunoko* is salted. To eat, some of the salt is removed by soaking in water. The roe is then dipped in a stock flavored with soy sauce. *Kazunoko* forms an important part of the New Year menu.

kegani けがに 毛蟹 horse-hair crab *Erimacrus isenbeckii*. Especially prolific around Hokkaido, this crab has tender meat that is a great delicacy. The shell is from 9 to 13 cm wide. Sold either boiled or live, it is usually eaten boiled and dipped in **sanbaizu**.

kenchinjiru けんちんじる 巻繊汁 vegetable soup. *Kenchin* refers to an assembly of chopped vegetables and tofu. Finely chopped carrot, burdock, white radish, and mushrooms are sautéed in a little oil with crumbled tofu that has been well squeezed of water. The soup is completed with the addition of **dashi**, salt, and soy sauce.

keshinomi けしのみ　芥子の実、罌粟の実　opium-poppy seed *Papaver somniferum*. An ingredient of **shichimi tōgarashi**, poppy seeds are also used for decoration. Those used in Japan are usually quite pale, almost white in color.

kezuribushi けずりぶし　削り節　shaved **katsuobushi**. It is often sold in plastic bags in supermarkets under the name *hanagatsuo* はながつお　花鰹. *See also* Appendix 2.

kibi きび　黍、稷　proso millet *Panicum mileaceum*. Very similar to **awa** in most respects, it is slightly more nutritious. It is sometimes cooked with rice, or mixed with glutinous rice to make **mochi**. The flour is used to make **dango**, a speciality of Okayama City.

kihada きはだ　黄肌　yellowfin tuna *Thunnus albacares*. A large fish, growing up to 3 m in length and 200 kg in weight, its best season is summer to autumn, when it approaches the shores of Japan. Its flavor is not as good as that of **maguro**. It is eaten as sushi, sashimi, and teriyaki.

kiji きじ　雉、雉子　pheasant *Phasianus versicolor*. The female pheasant is a protected bird and most of the pheasant available for eating in Japan is either farmed or imported. It is eaten as **yakimono**, **agemono**, and in soups.

kiku きく　菊　chrysanthemum *Chrysanthemum* spp. The leaves are used as the vegetable **shungiku** and the leaves and small flowers as a garnish. Large flowers of varieties such as *abōkyū* 阿房宮 are blanched and served in **sunomono**.

kikurage きくらげ　木耳　Jew's ear, cloud ear fungus *Auricularia auricula*. A tree fungus prized more for its gelatinous texture than its almost nonexistent flavor. It is dried and reconstituted in warm water for use. Sliced thinly, it is used in **sunomono**, **aemono**, and **o-hitashi**.

kinako きなこ　黄粉　parched soybean flour. *See also* **daizu**.

kine きね　杵　pestle. Whether large for use with **usu** or small for use with **suribachi**, Japanese pestles are made of wood. Because of its extreme hardness, the wood of the prickly ash (**sanshō**) is prized for the small braying pestles called **surikogi**.

kinkan きんかん 金柑 kumquat *Fortunella* spp. Many species of this attractive small citrus fruit are cultivated. They are eaten raw and also made into all kinds of sugar preserves, jams, jellies, and marmalade. A December-to-February fruit.

kinoko きのこ 茸 mushroom.

kinome きのめ 木の芽 young leaves of **sanshō**. *See also* **sanshō**.

kinpira gobō きんぴらごぼう 金平牛蒡 burdock dish. Burdock is shaved or sliced into matchsticks, shallow-fried, and seasoned with sugar, chili pepper, saké, and soy sauce. Carrot can be prepared the same way or mixed with burdock.

kinton きんとん 金団 sweet confection of chestnuts and sweet potato. Sweet potato (**satsumaimo**) is made into a sweetened purée, which can be molded to look like chestnuts. Whole and crumbled chestnuts can be added to the purée, which is then eaten with a spoon. This is a festive dish popular at New Year.

kinugoshidōfu きぬごしどうふ 絹漉し豆腐 *See* **tōfu**.

kiriboshi daikon きりぼしだいこん 切干し大根 *See* **daikon**.

kiritanpo きりたんぽ 切りたんぽ rice grilled on a skewer. The name comes from the practice spear (*tanpo*). New rice is cooked a little on the hard side and then pounded to a paste, which is molded around "spears" of cedar and grilled at the **irori**. When done, the grilled rice is eaten with a vegetable soup made with chicken stock. A speciality of Akita Prefecture.

kisetsu ryōri きせつりょうり 季節料理 seasonal cookery. Seasonality is very important in Japanese food culture and each season has representative food symbols and garnishes. A decoration of ginkgo or persimmon leaves indicates the autumn, pine needles and **ume** blossoms, New Year and early spring. The various fish, so long as they are fresh, are also clear markers of the seasons.

kishimen きしめん　棊子麺　flat wheat noodles. A speciality of Nagoya, this kind of **udon** is long, wide, flat, and thin.

kisu きす　鱚　sand borer, Japanese whiting *Sillago japonica*. This whiting can grow up to 30 cm but generally is much smaller. It is a tasty fish, better in summer, that is eaten in many ways.

kitsune udon きつねうどん　狐饂飩　*See* **udon**.

kobucha こぶちゃ　昆布茶　kelp tea, made when boiling water is poured onto dried, powdered **konbu**. *See also* Appendix 12.

kochi こち　鯒　flathead *Platycephalus indicus*. This fish, which can grow up to 50 cm or so, can be delicious and is very good as sashimi. It also makes good tempura, **suimono**, and **nimono**. At its best in March and April.

kohada こはだ　小鰭　local Tokyo name for young **konoshiro** about 15 cm long.

koi こい　鯉　carp *Cyprinus carpio*. The common carp grows to 30 or more cm, even up to 1 m. It is tastiest in winter and is very good in **miso shiru**, which cloaks its smell. For sashimi, carp is prepared as **arai**, but there is a danger of parasite infection from eating it raw.

kōika こういか　甲烏賊　cuttlefish *Sepiia esculenta*. Inhabiting the more southerly waters of Japan, it has a body about 18 cm long, with another 20 cm for the tentacles. From the food point of view, it can be treated the same as **ika**.

kōji こうじ　麹　rice, barley, or soybeans infected with the mold (*kabi*) called *Aspergillus oryzae*. It is used in the manufacture of saké, soy sauce, miso, **mirin**, **shōchū**, and **nattō**.

komatsuna こまつな　小松菜　mustard spinach *Brassica campestris* var. *perviridis*. Despite its English name, *komatsuna* is more like a leafy turnip than either mustard or spinach, though it does bear a superficial resemblance to the latter. One of the few purely Japanese vegetables, it has been cultivated in Japan from ancient times but it is rarely seen elsewhere. It is a favorite winter vegeta-

KOMATSUNA

ble rich in calcium and can be used in any way green vegetables are used.

kome こめ 米 rice (harvested but uncooked) *Oryza sativa* subsp. *japonica*. The rice grown and eaten in Japan is the short-grained subspecies *japonica*. It may be non-glutinous (*uruchimai* 粳米) or glutinous (**mochigome** 糯米).

komebitsu こめびつ 米櫃 rice bin or chest. Traditionally a wooden box, it is nowadays usually made of metal or plastic.

komugi こむぎ 小麦 wheat *Triticum aestivum*. Wheat is used in the manufacture of soy sauce and miso. Wheat flour has many uses, including the batter for tempura and cakes such as **kasutera**.

kona wasabi こなわさび 粉山葵 wasabi powder. Although a very small amount of true **wasabi** is made into a powder, the great bulk of *wasabi* powder is not *wasabi* at all, but powdered horseradish with green coloring and some mustard powder. Even when the paste is made up and sold in tubes, only the more expensive ones have any real *wasabi* in them. Since the shelf life of these better ones is short, they are not widely sold, and tubes of pure *wasabi* are not exported at all. If the tube says 100% fresh *wasabi*, buy it and taste the difference! *See also* Appendix 16.

konbu こんぶ 昆布 kelp *Laminaria* spp. The importance of this seaweed in Japanese food life can scarcely be overestimated. It

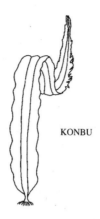

KONBU

is essential for making **dashi** stock and is used in innumerable other ways in cooking. *Konbu* requires cold water and grows off the coasts of northern Japan, especially Hokkaido, where *rausu konbu* 羅臼昆布, for making *dashi*, and *rishiri konbu* 利尻昆布, for general use, are cultivated and harvested in vast quantities at the end of summer. The *konbu* is dried and cut into lengths of 1 m or more for sale. Specialist shops sell it in such lengths, but supermarkets have to sell it in shorter lengths or folded up. Shredded *konbu* can be fried and eaten as **agemono** or **itamemono**, and shaved *konbu*, previously soaked in vinegar, is used for making **tororo konbu** and **oboro konbu**. *Konbu tsukudani* is very popular and *o-shaburi konbu* is chewed, a traditional alternative to gum. *Konbu* is enormously rich in monosodium glutamate, for which *see also* Appendix 14.

kondate こんだて　献立　menu. The term is especially used for formalized traditional menus such as that of **cha kaiseki**.

konnyaku こんにゃく　蒟蒻、蒟蒻　elephant foot, devil's tongue *Amorphophallus rivieri* var. *konjac*. A gelatinous paste is made from the root of this plant and either formed into bricks or strings. The bricks are usually eaten in simmered dishes, whole in **o-den**, sliced or broken up in other dishes. A white form is sliced thinly and served as a vegetarian sashimi called **yama fugu**. Thin strings (**shirataki**) are used in sukiyaki, and a thicker string is called *ito konnyaku*. Konnyaku is eaten for its chewy texture rather than its flavor. It should always be briefly boiled before use.

kō no mono こうのもの　香の物　pickle. A formal name for **tsu-kemono**.

konoshiro このしろ　鰶、鯯　gizzard shad *Clupanodon punctatus*. A large saraine, growing up to 25 cm. A profusion of small bones makes it troublesome to eat. At its best in autumn, it is eaten as sashimi, sushi, **sunomono**, and **shioyaki**. In Tokyo the smaller 15-cm fish is called **kohada**.

konowata このわた　海鼠腸　fermented sea-slug (**namako**) intestines. This is one of the three delicacies of the Edo period (1603–1868). It can be eaten with a little grated **yuzu** peel or mixed with grated **daikon** or chopped quail's egg. Usually served as a food with drinks (**sakana 1**). *See also* **karasumi**.

konpeitō コンペイトー　金平糖　comfit. A sugar candy introduced by the Portuguese in the sixteenth century, one kind of **higashi**. It is a small toffee sphere (5 mm in diameter) with a pimply surface, made from sugar, water, and flour, in a variety of colors. Originally there was a sesame seed in the middle, later a poppy seed, but nowadays no seed at all. The word comfit derives from the Portuguese *confeito*, meaning confection.

konro こんろ　焜炉　portable cooking stove. Charcoal-burning stoves have largely been replaced by gas and electric rings.

koromo ころも　衣　batter and other food coverings and dressings. Tempura batter, egg and bread crumbs for **furai**, the dressing for **aemono**, as well as a dusting of sugar are all classed as *koromo*. However, outside the professional sphere the word *koromo* is used only for the batter of tempura.

koshiki こしき　漉し器　sieve. Horsehair sieves are available, but usually the mesh is nylon or metal. Also called **uragoshi**.

KUCHINASHI

kōshinryō こうしんりょう　香辛料　spice. Among the traditional Japanese spices are **asanomi**, hemp seeds; **goma**, sesame; **karashi**, mustard; **keshinomi**, poppy seeds; **sanshō** and **kinome**, prickly-ash seeds and leaves; **shōga**, ginger; **tōgarashi**, chili pepper; **wasabi**, horseradish; and **yuzu**, Japanese citron.

koshō こしょう　胡椒　pepper. Not commonly used in Japanese cooking, but mixed with salt (*shiokoshō*) it is sprinkled on deep-fried chicken.

kōsō こうそう　香草　herb. The main Japanese herbs are **benitade**, water pepper; **seri**, water dropwort; **shiso**, perilla; and **mitsuba**, trefoil. *See also* **sansai ryōri** and **nanakusagayu**.

kowameshi こわめし　強飯　steamed glutinous rice. The best-known dish of this kind is **o-kowa**, also called **sekihan**. It is a celebratory dish that was originally made with red rice (*akamai* 赤米, usually non-glutinous in Japan). Glutinous rice steamed with other things such as salmon and **sansai** is often sold in department stores and is also called *o-kowa*.

kōyadōfu こうやどうふ　高野豆腐　"freeze-dried" tofu. When tofu is frozen and thawed, it becomes very spongy. After it has thawed, it is dried and then reconstituted in water for use. Being spongy, it is a good absorber of flavors. It is much used in **maki-zushi** and **shōjin ryōri**.

kuchinashi くちなし　梔子　gardenia *Gardenia jasminoides*. The flowers, which bloom in June and July, are used as a garnish for sashimi. The dried pods are used for an orange-red coloring for such things as **takuanzuke** and sweet-potato **kinton**.

kujira くじら　鯨　whale *Balaenoptera* spp.; *Balaena* spp. Whale meat is available in some markets and there are restaurants that specialize in whale-meat dishes, notably one at Shibuya in Tokyo.

kurage くらげ　水母、　海月　jellyfish 1. echizen kurage (*Stomolophus nomurai*) 2. bizen kurage (*Rhopilema esculenta*). The Echizen jellyfish, about 1 m in diameter, is about twice the size of the Bizen. Jellyfish is salted and then dried in the sun. It is mostly used in **sunomono** after the salt is soaked out. Having little if any flavor, *kurage* is enjoyed for its crunchiness.

kuri くり　栗　chestnut *Castanea crenata*. Chestnuts are greatly enjoyed in Japan and used in many sweet confections such as **kinton**. However, the local chestnut is very difficult to peel and most of the chestnuts consumed are imported from China. **Amaguri** (sweet chestnuts) are made by roasting chestnuts in a tub of revolving hot pebbles. Brown sugar or syrup is added to increase the sweetness by permeating the skin and at the same time makes the skin easier to remove with the fingernails. This is especially useful since *amaguri* are often sold in places of outdoor leisure.

kuri kinton くりきんとん　栗金団　*See* **kinton**.

kurodai くろだい　黒鯛　black bream, black porgy *Acanthopagrus schlegeli*. Growing about 40 cm long, it is at its best in April. It is not suitable for sashimi because of its "marine" smell, but is extremely good as **shioyaki**.

kuromame くろまめ　黒豆　black soybeans *Glycine max*. Sold in the dried form, these beans are soaked, boiled till tender, and sweetened. An essential ingredient of the New Year **o-sechi ryōri**.

kuruma ebi くるまえび　車海老　tiger prawn *Penaeus japonicus*. *See also* **ebi**.

kurumi くるみ　胡桃　common walnut *Juglans regia*. Walnut paste makes a delicious **koromo** for **aemono**. Otherwise, walnuts are extensively used in confectionary, usually broken into small pieces.

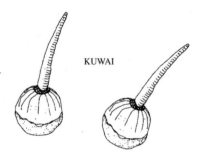

KUWAI

kushi くし 串 skewer. Fish are carefully skewered for grilling on metal skewers. Bamboo skewers are used for **yakitori**, *kushiyaki* (skewer grilling), and the extremely tasty *kushiage*, in which all kinds or ingredients are coated with egg and bread crumbs, skewered, and deep-fried.

kuwai くわい 慈姑 arrowhead *Sagittaria trifolia* var. *edulis*. This plant, which grows in shallow water, has a bulb 3 to 5 cm in diameter, with a pointed protuberance about 4 cm long. To eat, it is peeled, boiled, and seasoned. It is often served as **nimono** and features in the New Year **o-sechi ryōri**. *Kuwai* is rich in protein and has a somewhat waxy texture.

kuzu くず 葛 kudzu *Pueraria lobata*. A high-quality thickening starch is made from this vine. The starch is made in many parts or Japan but the most famous *kuzu* comes from Yoshino in Nara Prefecture. It is used to make sesame tofu (**goma dofu**) and a kind of **sōmen** and has many other uses.

kyōdo ryōri きょうどりょうり 郷土料理 local cuisine. There is an enormous variety of local styles of cooking throughout Japan, hardly surprising when the great variations in climate and other local differences are considered.

kyōna きょうな 京菜 pot herb mustard *Brassica campestris* var. *lanciniifolia*. A versatile green leaf vegetable associated with Kyoto. It is closely related to **mizuna** and has beautiful, shiny, feathery leaves growing in clumps. May be used in soups and pickles as well as **aemono**, **nimono**, and **nabemono**.

kyō ryōri きょうりょうり　京料理 Kyoto cuisine. Kyoto was not only the capital of Japan for many centuries, but was (and still is) the home of Buddhism. This meant that not only did high-class, elegant cookery such as **cha kaiseki** flourish, but so also did **shōjin ryōri**, the Buddhist vegetarian cuisine. In fact, vegetables, especially pickles, are a notable feature of Kyoto's food culture, not least because the city was too far from the sea to get good fish in the days before refrigeration. Kyoto is also famous for its elegant **bentō** and its high-quality **higashi**.

kyūri きゅうり　胡瓜 cucumber *Cucumis sativus*. Japanese cucumbers are small and without the coarse seeds that are such a drawback of the Western cucumber. They can be eaten raw, but are usually prepared as **sunomono** or **tsukemono**.

kyūsu きゅうす　急須 teapot. Mainly used for serving **sencha**, it is a small pot made of pottery or china, with a lug for a handle, or no handle at all. *See also* **cha**.

—M—

ma- ま-　真- prefix meaning true, proper. It is often attached to the most representative species of an animal or plant, e.g., *ma-aji* and *ma-konbu*.

mabikina まびきな　間引菜 young shoots (cotyledon) of green vegetables and herbs. **Kaiware** is one kind of *mabikina*.

maguro まぐろ　鮪 tunny, tuna, bluefin tuna *Thunnus thynnus*. A very large fish, growing to between 1 m and 3 m and up to 700 kg or more in weight. At its best in June but very good at any time, it makes superb sashimi and sushi. The pale ventral meat (**toro**), rich in oil, is the most highly regarded. If *maguro* has to be cooked,

MAITAKE

then **shioyaki** and teriyaki are the best ways, though it is also good as **nimono**.

maitake まいたけ 舞茸 hen-of-the-woods fungus *Grifola frondosa*. An autumn fungus, it is very fragrant, truly delicious, versatile, popular, and extensively cultivated. It is also more suitable for Western cooking than most Japanese mushrooms, being very good in an omelet. In Japanese cookery, it goes well in rice dishes, soups, and **nimono**. Best of all is *maitake no kurumi ae*, a dressed salad (**aemono**) with walnut paste as the **koromo**.

makisu まきす 巻き簾 bamboo mat for rolling sushi.

makizushi まきずし 巻き鮨 sushi roll. With a filling of **kanpyō**, **mitsuba**, omelet, mushrooms, and **kōyadōfu**, sushi rice is rolled in a sheet of **nori** with a **makisu**. This is cut into thick slices and eaten as is or dipped in soy sauce.

makunouchi bentō まくのうちべんとう 幕の内弁当 boxed meal originally for eating in the intervals between Kabuki plays. It has become a good standard **bentō** for any occasion, in which rice, sprinkled with sesame seeds, is accompanied by a variety of tidbits, usually ten or more different kinds.

mame まめ 豆 bean. The term includes peas, but above all refers to the soybean.

mame moyashi まめもやし 豆萌やし、豆蘖 bean sprouts. The commonest ones are those made from mung beans (**ryokutō**), but the larger sprouts of soybeans are also readily available. *Moyashi* are extensively used in **tsukemono** and **nabemono**.

MAKIZUSHI

managatsuo まながつお 真魚鰹、鯧 silver pomfret, butterfish *Pampus argenteus*. An excellent food fish, at its best in winter. It grows to a length of about 50 cm. Best eaten as sashimi, it is also prepared as teriyaki and **misozuke**. It is widespread in the waters of southern Asia.

manaita まないた 俎板、俎 chopping board. The traditional Japanese ones were (and still are) on two horizontal struts.

manjū まんじゅう 饅頭 sweet bun. Usually steamed, leavened wheat- or rice-flour buns filled with **an** (*anman*), pork (*butaman*), or even curry (*karēman*). A very popular snack sold and eaten hot. These buns are the same as some kinds of Chinese dim sum.

marumero マルメロ quince *Cydonia oblonga*. This is the European and Middle Eastern quince, introduced into Japan about 1620. Its uses are the same as those for **karin** but it does not have the same astringency. The Japanese word is derived from the Portuguese *marmelo*, meaning quince.

maruyaki まるやき 丸焼き grilling in the piece. This can refer to anything from a whole chicken to a whole pig, indeed anything that has not been cut up.

masu 1. ます 鱒 cherry salmon, masu salmon, sakuramasu *Oncorhynchus masou masou*. The sea-run form of this fish is predominant in northern Japan, whereas the freshwater form (**yamame**) is predominant in western Japan. *Masu* attains about 60 cm and about 15 kg and is a very good eating fish, cooked in any of the ways salmon is cooked. **Shioyaki** is very good.

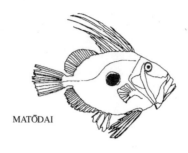

MATŌDAI

masu 2. ます 枡、升 measure for volume; and for drinking saké. Traditionally these were wooden boxes of standard size. They have been supplemented with metal and plastic cups.

matcha まっちゃ 抹茶 powdered green tea. *See also* Appendices 12 and 13.

matōdai まとうだい 的鯛 John Dory *Zeus faber*. This excellent eating fish attains 50 cm and is found south of Fukushima Prefecture. It has an enormous mouth and a big black spot on its side. It is best in winter and is very good as teriyaki and **misozuke**.

matsubagani まつばがに 松葉蟹 matsuba crab, Pacific snow crab, queen crab *Chionoecetes opilio*. This is the San'in (western Japan on the Japan Sea side) name for **zuwaigani**.

matsutake まつたけ 松茸 matsutake fungus *Tricholoma matsutake*. For those who can afford it, eating good-quality *matsutake* in autumn is one of the great experiences of life. It is very good in rice, even better in **dobinmushi**, and some say grilled in foil, best of all. There is a certain ribaldry about young men and women going hunting for *matsutake*, since it is quite phallic in shape, and the chances of getting lost in the woods of red pine where it grows are quite high. *Matsutake* is very hard to find and is imported on a large scale, especially from Korea.

mebaru めばる 眼張 rockfish, Japanese stingfish *Sebastes inermis*. Found in the coastal waters all around Japan, it attains a

MATSUTAKE

length of 30 cm and is best to eat in March. It is prepared as **ni-tsuke**, teriyaki, and **kara-age**.

mejina めじな　眼仁奈　large-scale blackfish, luderick *Girella punctata*. Very similar in appearance to black bream but at 50 cm a bit larger, it is a coastal fish found from Hokkaido to the East China Sea. Tastiest in winter, it is best eaten as sashimi, **shioyaki**, and **nitsuke**.

menbō めんぼう　麺棒　rolling pin. The long (1-m) thin ones for rolling noodles are best made of oak.

menma メンマ　麺碼、支那竹　*See* **shinachiku**.

men rui めんるい　麺類　noodles. Noodles form a significant part of Japanese food culture. Various kinds are available, the main ones being **udon**, **soba**, **rāmen**, **kishimen**, and **sōmen**.

mentai めんたい　明太　*See* **suketōdara**.

mentaiko めんたいこ　明太子　Alaska pollack roe. A speciality of Hakata in Kyushu, the roe is salted and flavored with chili pepper. It is usually colored a deep red. Also called *karashimentai* or *karashimentaiko*, the *karasni* being **tōgarashi**.

meshi めし　飯　informal word for cooked rice or a meal.

mikan みかん　蜜柑　mandarin, tangerine *Citrus unshiu*. Frequently but mistakenly referred to as *Citrus reticulata*, which in Japanese is **ponkan**. Mandarins are a very popular winter fruit and are consumed in vast quantities as a snack.

MIRUKUI (MIRUGAI)

mirin みりん 味醂 sweet liquid flavoring. It is made by mixing steamed glutinous rice on which rice mold, *Aspergillus oryzae*, has developed, with **shōchū** (distilled spirits). In forty to sixty days sweetness develops, the resulting liquid containing 14% alcohol. It is exclusively used in cooking, for its sweetness rather than its alcoholic flavor. Regular saké is no substitute and it is incorrect and misleading to call *mirin* "a kind of sweet cooking saké." It is important to distinguish between genuine *mirin* and low-alcohol imitation *mirin*. The real thing, *hon mirin*, is sold at saké shops and good supermarkets.

mirinboshi みりんぼし 味醂干し small fish such as **kisu**, **aji**, and **iwashi** flattened open, seasoned with a marinade of **mirin**, soy sauce, and sugar, and then dried. Sometimes sesame seeds are sprinkled over them. They make a good **tsumamimono**, and are the better for being lightly grilled.

mirugai みるがい 海松貝、水松貝 mirugai clam, gaper *Tresus keenae*. Sometimes incorrectly called **bakagai**, this clam-shaped bivalve is about 14 cm across and 9 cm thick. A large syphon projects from the shell. It is prevalent in all the shallow waters around Japan. The syphon is eaten, after being skinned, as sushi, sashimi, and **sunomono**. It is very chewy. The intestines, adductor muscle, and foot are also eaten but are inferior in flavor. The name *mirugai* is a popular misnomer for **mirukui**.

mirukui みるくい 海松食、水松食 the correct name for **mirugai**. *Mirukui* means eater of sea staghorn, a seaweed (*Codium fragile*), *miru* in Japanese, because that is what this shellfish does.

miso みそ　味噌　miso is a fermented paste of soybeans and usually either barley or rice, with salt. Its prototype came to Japan from the Asian mainland sometime between the sixth and seventh centuries. Miso is an essential Japanese foodstuff that is highly nutritious and is not only a basic of cooking, above all in miso soup, but is also often used as a flavoring. Both in taste and aroma, miso is highly savory, almost meaty, having about 14% high-quality protein and 5 to 12% salt. *See also* Appendix 6.

misoni みそに　味噌煮　long gentle simmering with miso. It is a kind of a **nimono**, and is especially used with fish such as **ei** and **saba**.

miso shiru みそしる　味噌汁　miso soup. In this basic Japanese soup, **dashi** is thickened with miso, and fish, vegetables, and such things as tofu are added. It is not necessary to use the best *dashi*, and **awasemiso** is considered to give the best flavor. Shellfish in the shell and fish on the bone are used, and the vegetables should not throw off scum, as burdock does. Tofu, **kōyadōfu**, and **abura-age** go well, as do both fresh and dried **fu**. Miso soup is essential to a Japanese breakfast and is served at most other meals as well. It is a good source of protein, especially in conjunction with the eating of rice.

misozuke みそづけ　味噌漬け　miso pickles. Suitably sized whole vegetables and fish or meat are pickled in a bed of miso, the length of time varying from a couple of hours to as much as a month. The vegetables are eaten as pickles (**tsukemono**), and the fish or meat is grilled or cooked in other ways.

mitarashi dango みたらしだんご　御手洗団子　rice-flour **dango**. These balls are a speciality of the Shimokamo shrine in Kyoto. Five balls are put on a skewer and grilled with a basting of soy sauce. The ball at the tip, representing a human head, is larger than the others, which are the body. They are given as offerings at weddings at the shrine.

MITSUBA

mitsuba みつば　三つ葉　trefoil, Japanese wild chervil *Crypto-taenia japonica*. *Mitsuba* is used as herb in soups, salads, and with vinegared and fried foods. It derives its name, literally three leaves in Japanese, from the three leaflets that make up the leaf. It is very similar in appearance to **seri** and coriander (not used in Japanese cooking at all) but totally different in its flavor, which is that of a mild chervil.

mitsumame みつまめ　蜜豆　popular sweet dish. Various things, including small pieces of fruit and sweet beans, are placed in a bowl with cubes of **kanten**. Syrup, either clear or dark, is poured over the top. When the **an** of **azuki** is included, it is called **an-mitsu**.

mizuame みずあめ　水飴　glucose (syrup). Used in making candies and jam.

mizuna みずな　水菜　pot herb mustard *Brassica campestris* var. *lanciniifolia*. *See also* **kyōna**.

mizutaki みずたき　水炊き　chicken **nabemono**. Roughly chopped chicken on the bone (**butsugiri**) is simmered in a communal pot with seasonal vegetables and such things as tofu and bean sprouts. When ready, they are dipped in **ponzu** and eaten. Lastly **mochi** or **udon** may be simmered in the delicious remaining stock.

mochi もち　餅　rice cake. Glutinous rice is steamed, pounded into a paste, and shaped into cakes. Traditionally, in eastern Japan the cakes are cut with a knife (*kirimochi*), in western Japan they are shaped into circles by hand. In recent years this distinction has become less clear-cut. In either case they are eaten as is while still soft, and when they become hard are toasted and served in many ways, such as with **nori** or soy sauce or sugar. They are one of the essential Japanese foods, and having a celebratory significance, are particularly eaten at New Year, when many people try to eat a lot of them. They are served in **zōni**, the special New Year soup. They are very soft and sticky and every year a number of people, usually old people, choke to death on them.

mochigome もちごめ　糯米　glutinous rice *Oryza sativa* subsp. *japonica* Glutinosa Group. The regular rice eaten by the Japanese is not, as is so often stated, glutinous rice, but non-glutinous rice (*uruchimai*). Glutinous rice is largely reserved for special occasions and has to be steamed in a steamer. The principal glutinous-rice preparation, apart from all kinds of **mochi**, is **sekihan**.

momendōfu もめんどうふ　木綿豆腐　*See* **tōfu**.

monaka もなか　最中　stuffed wafer cake. A kind of **wagashi**, dating from the early nineteenth century, in which rice is made into a very light wafer, which is stuffed with **an**. There is a variety of shapes and sizes and also of the kinds of *an* used.

moriawase もりあわせ　盛り合わせ　*See* **moritsuke** 5, *mazemori*.

morijio もりじお　盛り塩　pile of salt. From the earliest times salt has been associated with ritual purity in Japan, and little piles of salt have been placed at shrines to purify and gain the gods' protective presence. The Grand Shrine of Ise, finding modern salt quite unsatisfactory for this purpose, has maintained its own salt terrace (*mishiohama* 御塩浜) to produce salt in the traditional way. A quite different custom is found in entertainment districts, where *morijio* is sometimes placed outside the entrance to a bar, and is intended to attract customers to enter. The custom originated in China with carriage oxen stopping to lick the salt. *See also* Appendix 8.

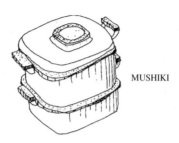

MUSHIKI

moritsuke もりつけ 盛り付け food arrangement. There are basically seven formalized ways of arranging food on a plate, governed by the foods to be arranged and the vessels to be used. The seven are 1. *sugimori*, strips and slices of food in a slanting pile; 2. *kasanemori*, slices placed overlapping each other; 3. *tawaramori*, blocks or rounds placed horizontally in a pyramid; 4. *hiramori*, flat slices of sashimi arranged vertically; 5. *mazemori*, a mixed pile of different-colored thin strips. (Also, with foods such as **nigirizushi**, a representative selection arranged on a plate. For *nigirizushi*, *see also* Appendix 11.); 6. *yosemori*, two or three contrasting ingredients arranged next to each other; 7. *chirashimori*, like *yosemori* but with space between the ingredients. Less common than these seven is *takamori* in which the ingredients are piled high above the vessel. It is nowadays restricted to service of the gods and the emperor. *See also* **ōmori**.

morokyū もろきゅう sliced cucumber spread with **moromi** of soy sauce. **Hishio**, when available, is often used instead of *moromi*. So also is *kinzanji miso*, for which *see also* Appendix 6. **Morokyū** is served as **tsumamimono** or **zensai**.

moromi もろみ 1. 醪 unfiltered saké. 2. 諸味 unfiltered soy sauce. In both cases *moromi* refers to the product at a stage prior to filtration. Soy-sauce *moromi* has several uses in cooking.

moromi miso もろみみそ 諸味味噌 chopped, salt-pickled vegetables are added to **moromi** 2 made with less water than usual, and miso starter mold, *Aspergillus oryzae*, is added. The final

MYŌGA

product is dark brown in color and soft in consistency, and mostly eaten on slices of cucumber.

motsu もつ giblets, entrails. *Motsunabe* is a kind of **nabemono** in which several kinds of viscera are used.

moyashi もやし 萌やし、蘖 *See* **mame moyashi**.

mozuku もずく 水雲、海蘊 mozuku *Nemacystis decipiens*. A dark brown seaweed with filaments 30 to 40 cm long, which is preserved in salt and eaten as **tsumamimono**. It also makes very good **sunomono**.

mugi むぎ 麦 grain. Wheat, barley, oats, and rye are all *mugi*, but without qualification *mugi* generally means barley. *Mugicha* is a refreshing infusion of roasted barley, very popular as an iced drink in summer. *See also* Appendix 12.

mugi kogashi むぎこがし 麦焦がし parched barley flour. *See also* **ōmugi**.

mukōzuke むこうづけ 向こう付け first course. This is the **namasu** or sashimi of **kaiseki ryōri**. The Japanese word refers to the position of the dish on the tray, opposite the bowls of rice and soup.

murasaki むらさき 紫 soy sauce. A sushi-shop word basically meaning purple.

muroaji むろあじ 室鯵、鰘 brown-striped mackerel scad *Decapterus muroadsi*. This elegant fish attains a length of about 40 cm in the waters of western and southern Japan. It is eaten as sashimi and **shioyaki** and made into a kind of **himono** (dried fish) called *kusaya*.

mushiki むしき　蒸し器　steamer. The term generally refers to a modern-style metal steamer rather than the traditional wooden or bamboo **seirō**.

mushimono むしもの　蒸し物　steamed food. The best-known steamed dishes are **chawan mushi** and **tamago dōfu**. There are also many excellent dishes of steamed seafood. A particularly good refinement is *sakamushi*, in which saké is poured over the ingredients before steaming.

musubi 1. むすび　結び　a kind of knot or tie used to decorate food. Ingredients knotted include **kisu** and **mitsuba**.

musubi 2. むすび　結び　rice ball. Cold rice is formed into balls with a stuffing of something with a strong flavor, such as **bai niku**, **katsuobushi**, salmon, or chopped pickles. A strip of **nori** is often placed around the rice, or it can be sprinkled with sesame seeds. Rice balls are handy for picnics and school lunches. Also called *nigirimeshi* 握り飯 and popularly **o-nigiri** おにぎり.

mutsu むつ　鯥　Japanese bluefish *Scombrops boops*. This large-eyed, wide-mouthed fish, which attains up to 60 cm, is tastiest in very cold weather, when its fat content increases. It is eaten as sashimi, **nitsuke**, and teriyaki and is very good simmered in miso.

mutsugorō むつごろう　鯥五郎　blue spotted mud-hopper, pond-skipper *Boleophthalmus pectinirostris*. This fish is a kind of goby found in the coastal waters of western Japan. It grows to only about 15 cm in length, but in late spring and early summer, when its body fat increases, it is quite tasty grilled, particularly as **kabayaki**.

myōga みょうが　茗荷　mioga *Zingiber mioga*. Although mioga is a kind of ginger, it is scarcely recognizable as such, since only the buds and stems, not the rhizome, are eaten. The buds are very fragrant when thinly sliced and are used as a garnish. Both buds and stems are made into vinegar pickles, the pickled stems being used as a garnish for grilled fish in the same way that pickled ginger stems (**hajikami**) are used. Mioga is not hot like ginger, the fragrance being more herbal. Sliced, it makes an excellent addition to a salad.

—N—

nabe なべ　鍋　cooking pot or pan. There are metal ones of all shapes and sizes, including specialized pans for sukiyaki and **jingisukan nabe**, and earthenware ones such as the **donabe** for most other **nabemono**.

nabemono なべもの　鍋物　one-pot dish. A class of dishes cooked at table and served from the pot direct. These dishes have become popular since the adoption late last century of the **chabudai**. In a formal setting, they are still served individually, cooked on an individual **shichirin**.

nagaimo ながいも　長芋、　長薯　Chinese yam *Dioscorea opposita*. *See also* **yamanoimo**.

naganegi ながねぎ　長葱　a long variety of welsh onion valued for its large amount of white. *See also* **negi**.

nagasaki chanpon チャンポン　famous local dish of Nagasaki. A selection of pork, squid, prawns, oysters, and fish is fried in ample lard along with thinly sliced onion, carrot, cabbage, and other vegetables, and is then served in a large bowl containing lightly cooked Chinese noodles and soup made from roughly chopped pork and chicken on the bone.

nagashibako ながしばこ　流し箱　gelatin mold. A rectangular metal mold with insert for removing the jelly. Various **kanten** preparations, **goma dōfu**, and **tamago dōfu** are conveniently made in such a mold.

nama- なま-　生-　prefix meaning raw, fresh, not cooked in any way, e.g., **nama tamago**, raw egg.

nama-age なまあげ　生揚げ　*See* **atsuage**.

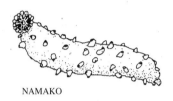

NAMAKO

namagashi なまがし 生菓子 uncooked sugar confection. *See also* **wagashi**.

namako なまこ 海鼠 sea slug, sea cucumber, holothurian *Stichopus japonicus* and *Cucumaria japonicus*. Sold live in markets, it is eaten raw in Japan, in contrast with China, where it is always dried. It is served as **sunomono** and is extremely hard and crunchy. It is not by any means liked by everyone and seems to have a greater appeal to the older generation. *Namako* intestines are fermented to make **konowata**.

namaribushi なまりぶし 生り節 "half-way" **katsuobushi**. Also called *namabushi*, this is *katsuobushi* with the process stopped at the smoking stage. It can be sliced with a knife. Since it still has a high water content, it does not keep very well, and is available only in places where *katsuobushi* is made. It is cut into blocks and served with vegetables as **nimono** and is also a very good **tsumamimono**.

namasu なます 膾、鱠、齏 vinegared dish of raw meat or fish. Whether meat, fish, or mixed is indicated by one of the three kanji shown above. The ingredients, which may include raw vegetables, are cut into thin strips and dressed with **nihaizu**, **sanbaizu**, sweet vinegar (*amazu* 甘酢), or **karashi sumiso**. **Daikon** is much used and so are oysters, which are not cut into thin strips.

namazu なまず 鯰 catfish *Silurus asotus*. A freshwater fish with a flat snout and two pairs of barbels. It grows to about 50 cm long

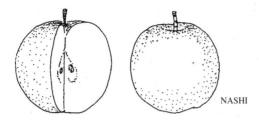

NASHI

and is low in fat and plain in flavor. It is grilled as **kabayaki** and served as tempura and in **miso shiru**.

nameko なめこ　滑子　nameko fungus *Pholiota nameko*. An autumn mushroom unique to Japan, it is golden brown in color and has a gelatinous coating much liked by the Japanese. *Nameko* does not keep very well and is usually bought in cans or salt-pickled in bottles. It is used in **miso shiru**, **nabemono**, and **aemono**.

nanairo tōgarashi なないろとうがらし　七色唐辛子　seven-color chili pepper. This is the Kanto (Tokyo area) name for **shichimi tōgarashi**.

nanakusagayu ななくさがゆ　七草粥、七種粥　seven-herb rice gruel. **O-kayu** flavored with the seven herbs of spring, which are **seri**, water dropwort; **nazuna**, shepherd's purse; **gogyō**, cudweed; **hakobe**, chickweed; **hotokenoza**, henbit; **suzuna** or **kabu**, turnip; and **suzushiro** or **daikon**, white radish. The gruel is eaten on January 7 to avoid all illness throughout the coming year, being regarded as a medicine. City dwellers can often buy little sets of the herbs in supermarkets.

nanbanzuke なんばんづけ　南蛮漬け　*escabèche*. Fried fish, such as **wakasagi** or small **aji**, pickled in vinegar flavored with chili pepper and welsh onion. The name *escabeche* means pickle in Portuguese, and the dish is found in Portugal, Spain, Provence, the Philippines, and many other places.

nanohana なのはな　菜の花　rape shoots *Brassica napus*. These are the immature stems of rape (colza) with their buds. Their appearance is remarkably similar to broccoli and they are used as a vegetable especially symbolizing spring. They are made into pickles and are particularly good as a cooked salad dressed with mustard (*nanohana no karashiae*).

naorai なおらい　直会　food and drink offered to the gods. Offering food to the gods is an important feature of religion in Japan, not as sacrifice but for spiritual communion. The food may be ordinary everyday items, but offerings at some temples and shrines, especially in Nara, include enormous displays of food that could never be eaten, at least by mortals, e.g., brightly colored uncooked rice.

narezushi なれずし　馴れ鮨、熟れ鮨　the most ancient form of sushi, which was a way of preserving fish rather than a way of eating rice. The best-known example is the *funazushi* from the Lake Biwa area near Kyoto, but the method is not unique to Japan, being found also in Korea and Southeast Asian countries. At Lake Biwa, **funa**, heavy with roe, are caught from late spring to early summer and salted. At the height of summer the salt is soaked out, and the fish are packed into large crocks between layers of cooked rice. The lids of the crocks are weighted down and the contents allowed to mature for up to six months. To eat, usually as **sakana 1**, the rice is removed and the fish sliced. The rice is normally discarded. *See also* Appendix 11.

nashi なし　梨　Japanese pear *Pyrus pyrifolia*. A popular autumn dessert fruit having the appearance and crispness of an apple but the juiciness and flavor of a pear. There are brown and green varieties, the brown having a slight flavor of caramel. *Shinkō* 新興 and *niitaka* 新高 are among the best brown varieties, and among the green, **nijisseiki** is very well known.

nasu なす　茄子　eggplant, aubergine *Solanum melongena*. Japanese eggplants do not have the bitterness of the larger Western ones and do not need to be salted before cooking. They make excellent tempura and are good shallow-fried and prepared with miso. Eggplant is also often used for **tsukemono**.

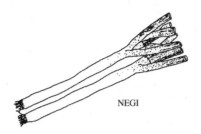

NEGI

natane なたね 菜種 rapeseed, colza *Brassica napus* and *Brassica campestris* var. *nippo-oleifera*. A good source of edible oil. Currently almost all rapeseed oil (canola oil) is imported.

natsume なつめ 棗 jujube, Chinese date *Zizyphus jujuba*. Jujubes, both dried and candied, have been imported from China since ancient times but are seldom encountered.

natsumikan なつみかん 夏蜜柑 Japanese summer orange, natsumikan *Citrus natsudaidai*. In season from spring to early summer, it is eaten raw and made into juice and marmalade.

nattō なっとう 納豆 fermented soybeans. Soaked and steamed soybeans are made up into little parcels with rice straw and inoculated with *Bacillus natto*. They are allowed to ferment for about a day in a hot, humid atmosphere and develop a strong aroma and flavor. They also develop a thready stickiness, noticeable when they are picked up with chopsticks. Usually *nattō* is served on top of hot rice, but is also used in **aemono** and **miso shiru**, in which it loses its threadiness and is very tasty.

nazuke なづけ 菜漬け salt pickles (**shiozuke**) made from **hiroshima na**, **kyōna**, **nozawana**, and **hakusai**. *See also* **tsukemono**.

nazuna なずな 齊 shepherd's purse *Capsella bursa-pastoris*. *See also* **nanakusagayu**.

negi ねぎ 葱 welsh onion, cibol, chibol *Allium fistulosum*. Somewhat similar to the leek (*Allium ampeloprasum* var. *porrum*) but thinner and much longer, it is used more as a condiment than as a vegetable. For the condiment **sarashi negi**, *negi* is sliced thinly, refreshed in iced water, drained, patted dry, and added to dips, especially for **nabemono**. *Negi* is also used in soups. As a vegetable it makes good **aemono** and is used in **yakimono**, especially **kushiyaki**. Note that welsh is spelled here with a small *w* to indicate the lack of connection with Wales. The word probably means foreign, though its origin is obscure.

nemagaritake ねまがりたけ　根曲がり竹 sasa bamboo, Chishima sasa *Sasa kurilensis*. The young shoots of this small variety of bamboo are one of the most popular items of **sansai ryōri**. They are served in many ways, especially **nitsuke**, sautéed, and used in **nabemono** and **aemono**.

neri- ねり-　練り- prefix meaning prepared in some way, especially by making into a paste and/or seasoning. *Neri-uni* and *neri-miso* are examples.

niboshi にぼし　煮干し small dried fish. Mostly very small anchovies (**katakuchi iwashi**), which are briefly boiled and dried. They are used for making **dashi** for **miso shiru**.

nigari にがり　苦汁 bittern. The residue, mostly magnesium chloride, of traditionally made sea salt was used as the coagulant of tofu. Now that it is scarcely available, other chemical coagulants are used.

nigirizushi にぎりずし　握り鮨 *See* Appendix 11.

nihaizu にはいず　二杯酢 vinegar and soy-sauce mix. The proportions are decided by taste, and the mixture is usually diluted with **dashi**.

nihonshu にほんしゅ　日本酒 saké. *See also* **saké 1**.

nijimasu にじます　　虹鱒 rainbow trout *Salmo gairdneri*. Introduced into Japan in 1877, it attains a length of 30 cm or so in the fluviatile form and up to 60 cm in the sea-run form. It is farmed all over Japan but is rarely found wild. The small fish are salt-grilled as **shioyaki** and the large ones are eaten as sashimi, sautéed, or baked or grilled in foil.

nijisseiki にじっせいき 二十世紀 one kind of Japanese pear, literally twentieth-century pear. *See also* **nashi**.

nikomi にこみ 煮込み food slowly simmered for a long time in a small amount of well-flavored stock. **O-den** is a well-known example.

niku にく 肉 meat. Beef is greatly enjoyed. *See also* **gyū niku** and **sukiyaki**. Pork is also eaten. *See also* **tonkatsu** and **tonkotsu**. Wild boar (**inoshishi**) and venison (*shika niku*) have been eaten since ancient times. Horse meat (*sakura niku*) is popular in some areas. *See also* **ba sashi**. Neither mutton, lamb, nor veal is used in the traditional Japanese cuisine.

nikujaga にくじゃが 肉じゃが a very popular kind of **nimono** with Western ingredients such as thinly sliced beef, potato, carrot, and onion.

nimono にもの 煮物 simmered food. A major category of Japanese cookery, *nimono* tends to appear in every meal except breakfast. It is one of the principal ways of serving vegetables and is also very useful in fish cookery. There are many different kinds of *nimono* according to the seasoning used. Saké, soy sauce, egg yolk, ginger, and miso are used as seasonings. Sweetening is done with **mirin** rather than sugar. Needed for *nimono* are a heavy, straight-sided pan and the drop-lid called **otoshibuta**.

ninjin にんじん 人参 carrot *Daucus carota*. Carrot has an important place among vegetables in Japan, where the orange-colored Western carrot and the reddish Japanese carrot are both in great demand. The Western carrot is available year-round but is best from early summer until autumn. The Japanese *takinogawa*, very long and thin, and *kintoki*, also fairly long but not so thin, are in season in the autumn and winter. Among their many uses, **nimono** is particularly important.

ninniku にんにく 大蒜、葫 garlic *Allium sativum*. Garlic is hardly used in authentic Japanese cookery, though it is always abundantly available. In **tataki** of beef or **katsuo** it is one of the herbs in the dip. It is also sometimes used in **gyōza**, instead of the usual **nira**.

nira にら　韮、韭　Chinese chives *Allium tuberosum*. *Nira* has a stronger, more garlicky aroma than Western chives. It is one of the ingredients of **gyōza** and can be used in soups, **o-hitashi**, and **itamemono**.

niru にる　煮る　to simmer, as in **nimono**.

nishime にしめ　煮染め　a kind of dry **nimono**, used in boxes of food such as **bentō** and **jūzume**. Fresh or dried vegetables, also fish and meat, are simmered until no liquid remains. The flavorings are ginger, **mirin**, and often soy sauce. *Nishime* has an important place among the foods of New Year, for which *see also* **o-sechi ryōri**.

nishin にしん　鰊　herring *Clupea pallasii*. This fish of the northern waters attains about 30 cm. At its tastiest in the spawning season from spring to early summer, it is prepared as **shioyaki** and **nimono**. The female roe is made into **kazunoko**.

nitsuke につけ　煮付け　sweet **nimono** primarily of fish, in which the ingredients are simmered with saké, **mirin**, and soy sauce until there is little remaining liquid.

niwatori にわとり　鶏　*See* **wakadori**.

nobiru のびる　野蒜　red garlic *Allium grayi*. Growing around the fringes of fields, it is picked in March and April for its bulbs, which can be eaten raw, or grilled and spread with miso. The leaves are also used in various ways.

noppei [jiru] のっぺい[じる]　能平[汁]、濃餅[汁]　thick soup that varies from region to region as part of **kyōdo ryōri**, and a favorite food at festivals. Ingredients such as carrot, **konnyaku**, taro, and **shiitake** are simmered in stock and flavored with soy sauce, salt, or some other flavoring. In some places chicken or fish is added.

nori のり　海苔　laver *Porphyra* spp. The red alga *asakusa nori* (*Porphyra tenera*) is the best-known species. When it is gathered, it is dried into sheets of a standard size (22.5 x 17.5 cm), which are packed in bundles of ten. This *nori* is toasted and used as wrapping for **norimaki**. The sheets are also further cut up and packed in different sizes, often in cellophane envelopes of five small toasted sheets suitable for wrapping around mouthfuls of rice at breakfast. This is called **yakinori**, or **ajitsuke nori**, when the small pieces are coated with spicy flavoring. Another *nori* is green laver, **aonori** (*Enteromorpha* spp.), which is dried and sold in small flakes to sprinkle on food. It grows on rocks in bays and at the mouths of rivers. This is sometimes confused with *hitoe-gusa* (*Monostroma nitidum*), which grows on rocks in dark areas lapped by the tide. *Hitoegusa* has a better flavor than *aonori*, and is made into **tsukudani**, sold as *tsukudani* of *nori* or sometimes of *iwanori*, which is actually either *Collema* spp. or *amanori* (*Por-phyra suborbiculata*). *Aonori* is one of the traditional ingredients of **shichimi tōgarashi**, but the cheaper *aosa*, あおさ 石蓴 *Ulva lactuca*, sea lettuce, is often used as a commercial substitute.

norimaki のりまき 海苔巻き sushi rolled up in sheets of **nori**. Sometimes the filling is quite simple, such as tuna or cucumber, but there are also quite elaborate fillings. *See also* **makizushi**.

nozawana のざわな 野沢菜 turnip greens *Brassica campestris* var. *hakabura*. A kind of **komatsuna** with large serrated leaves, which become sweeter and more tender with frost and snow. It is mostly made into **tsukemono**.

nukazuke ぬかづけ 糠漬け *See* **tsukemono**.

nukiita ぬきいた 抜き板 rectangular board supported on struts, which enable boards with food on them to be stacked on top of each other. This kind of board is also used to support grilled fish when the skewers are removed.

nuta ぬた 饅 **aemono** of fish and vegetables dressed with **sumiso** or **karashi sumiso**. Suitable ingredients are tuna, squid, shellfish, **wakame** seaweed, and welsh onion.

—O—

Notes: The honorific o- お 御 has been ignored in headings except in the few cases below where it seems an essential part of the word, such as **o-den** and **o-yaki**.

oboro おぼろ 朧 *See* **denbu**.

oboro konbu おぼろこんぶ 朧昆布 product very similar to **tororo konbu**, made from **konbu** that has been soaked in vinegar, dried, and shaved. It is best as **wandane** and in **sunomono**.

o-chazuke おちゃづけ 御茶漬け tea-flavored rice. Things such as fragments of salmon, shreds of **nori**, and pieces of **umeboshi**, all of which can come dried out of packets, are placed on a bowl of hot rice, and hot tea is poured over it. The dish is consumed with chopsticks, often after an evening's drinking.

o-den おでん 御田 hodgepodge. In a large container of hot **dashi**, a variety of ingredients is put to simmer. Among the favorites are potato, hard-boiled egg, **konnyaku**, **chikuwa**, tofu, **atsuage**, **daikon**, **hanpen**, and **konbu**, and in western Japan, chicken and octopus. *O-den* is served hot with a little stock and eaten with very hot mustard. It is considered a very plebeian dish. *O-den*'s full name is *nikomi dengaku*, and in the Kansai area, centering on Osaka, it is called *kantō daki* 関東炊き.

odorigui おどりぐい 躍り食い very small whitebait-like fish, such as **shirouo**, swallowed alive from stock flavored with vinegar and soy sauce. It is said that although the fish do not have much flavor, they cause an interesting feeling in the throat as they go down. *Odori* means dance, and *gui* or *kui* means eat.

o-hagi おはぎ 御萩 inside-out rice cake, so called because the **an** normally inside the cake is on the outside. The cake is named after *hagi* (bush clover), which flowers in the autumn and which the cake vaguely resembles. When these cakes are made in spring,

O-HITSU

they are called *botan mochi* (peony cakes). They are made with a mixture of glutinous and non-glutinous rice and are coated with *tsubuan*, for which *see also* **an**. Simple, very popular, and very good.

o-hitashi おひたし　御浸し　soused greens. Green vegetables such as **komatsuna**, **shungiku**, spinach, **hakusai**, or even bean sprouts are parboiled and soused in **dashi** seasoned with soy sauce and a little **mirin**. The dish should be served chilled.

o-hitsu おひつ　御櫃　rice-serving tub. A wooden tub, usually round, with a well-fitting lid, for bringing cooked rice to diners. It has largely been replaced, at least domestically, by the automatic rice cooker, which also keeps rice hot.

ohyō おひょう　大鮃　Pacific halibut *Hippoglossus stenolepis*. By far the largest of the flatfish, it measures from 1 to 2 m in length and can weigh up to 200 kg. It is a very lean fish and makes good sashimi and **agemono**. Also used for **kamaboko**.

o-jiya おじや　*See* **zōsui**.

o-kara おから　御殻　tofu lees. The bran of soybeans filtered out of the soy milk in the process of making tofu. It is also called *uno-hana* to avoid the unseemly connotation that *o-kara* has. Though not very tasty, it is extremely nutritious and can be dressed with shredded carrot, burdock, and so on to make it tolerable. Professionals sometimes use the term *kirazu* きらず　雪花菜.

o-kazu おかず　御数、御菜　*See* **sōzai**.

OKOZE

o-konomiyaki おこのみやき 御好み焼き savory pancake. *O-konomi* means your choice, so the customer chooses the filling of the pancake from a wide range of possibilities. Beef, squid, prawns, octopus, or pork is married with a flour-and-egg batter and cooked on a hot plate. Turning the large pancake over requires a modicum of skill, and there are two ways in which *o-konomiyaki* is prepared. In one, a cook makes it and serves it to the customer, and in the other, the customer cooks it for himself. When ready, the pancake is brushed with a thick, Japanese-style Worcester sauce and sprinkled with **aonori** and **katsuobushi**, then eaten with chopsticks and **ichimonji**.

o-kowa おこわ 御強 **sekihan** or other kind of **kowameshi**.

okoze おこぜ 虎魚 devil stinger *Inimicus japonicus* (**oni-okoze**). An appallingly ugly fish that tastes very good and is at its prime in summer. It attains a length of 20 cm and is eaten as sashimi and in soups.

ōmori おおもり 大盛り large serving. Plate or bowl piled high.

ōmugi おおむぎ 大麦 barley *Hordeum vulgare*. Used in the manufacture of miso and **shōchū**, and added to rice (before cooking) for added nutrition. For this purpose the grain is pressed, making it look remarkably like rolled oats. The refreshing summer drink *mugicha* is made from toasted barley, and a snack cereal is made by mixing hot water and sugar with parched barley flour, variously called *mugi kogashi*, *hattai* はったい 糗、麨, *hattaiko* はったい粉, or *kōsen* 香煎.

OROSHIGANE

o-musubi *See* **musubi 2**.

o-nigiri *See* **musubi 2**.

onomi おのみ 苧の実 hemp seed. An old name for **asanomi**.

oroshigane おろしがね 卸し金、下ろし金 grater. Strictly speaking, this refers to a grater made of metal, either steel or tinned copper. However, there are also pottery, wooden, and plastic graters. In all cases, there is a flat surface with sharp teeth protruding, and the grated matter collects on the grater. A special grater for **wasabi** has angel-shark skin (*korozame*) mounted on a piece of wood. It grates very finely but wears out quickly and is expensive. It is used for the most part only by sushi chefs.

o-sechi ryōri おせちりょうり　御節料理 New Year cuisine. The term covers a wide range of seasonal dishes but, above all, the foods arranged in the **jūbako**, consisting usually of four layers of cold foods, all of which have been invested with symbolism appropriate to the New Year. The top layer contains such celebratory foods as **kazunoko** and **kuromame**. The next down contains **kuri kinton**, **datemaki**, and the like. The third from the top contains seafood and more vegetables, preferably uncultivated ones such as **zenmai**. The bottom layer contains **nimono** of vegetables. The variation from family to family is considerable, and so is the expense, especially of shop-made *o-sechi*. People who do not have **jūzume** may serve individual dishes of such things as *kazunoko* and *kuromame*.

oshiki おしき　折敷 tray. This square tray is used specifically for the service of food directly on the tatami floor. In the days before the low communal table came into use, the square tray was used

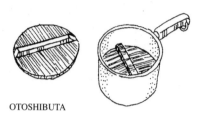

OTOSHIBUTA

by the common people, whereas the people of higher status used the small table called **zen**.

oshizushi おしずし 押し鮨 *See* Appendix 11.

o-tamajakushi おたまじゃくし 御玉杓子 soup ladle. Also called *o-tama* 御玉.

otoshibuta おとしぶた 落とし蓋 drop-lid. A wooden lid that drops onto what is cooking. An essential of cooking **nimono**, it keeps the vegetables from moving around and breaking up.

o-yaki おやき 御焼き an item of **kyōdo ryōri** of two distinct kinds. 1. In Nagano Prefecture a selection from among seasoned vegetables, pickles, and **an** wrapped up in a paste made of wheat flour, a mixture of wheat and buckwheat flours, or rice flour, and grilled or steamed. 2. In Yamanashi Prefecture **dango** made from boiled cornmeal and grilled.

oyako donburi おやこどんぶり 親子丼 *See* **donburi**.

o-yatsu おやつ 御八つ light meal, snack usually taken mid-afternoon.

—P—

panko パンこ パン粉 bread crumbs. Used mostly for **furai**, including **tonkatsu**, dried white crumbs, usually both fine and coarse, are sold in packets. In some shops, fresh crumbs are also available in cellophane packs.

pīman ピーマン capsicum, bell pepper, sweet pepper *Capsicum annuum* var. *grossum*. Sweet peppers, almost always green, are extensively used in such dishes as tempura, **yakiniku**, **nimono**, and **aemono**. The word *pīman* is derived from the French word *piment*, meaning bell pepper.

ponkan ポンカン 椪柑 ponkan-mandarin *Citrus reticulata*. Similar to **mikan** but larger, it weighs from 200 to 250 gm. It is eaten as a fresh fruit.

ponzu ポンず ポン酢 the juice of acidic citrus fruits such as **daidai**, **sudachi**, **kabosu**, or lemon. Most commonly, *ponzu* is an abbreviation for *ponzu jōyu*, a mixture of such juice and soy sauce, used as a dip for **mizutaki** and **chirinabe**.

—R—

rakkyō らっきょう 薤、辣韭 rakkyo, Baker's garlic *Allium chinense*. A kind or scallion very popular as a pickle. It is usually pickled either in sweetened vinegar or a mixture of **mirin** and soy sauce, and improves with keeping.

rāmen ラーメン 拉麺、老麺、柳麺 Chinese-style wheat noodles. Often called **chūka soba**, especially in western Japan, these noodles are served in many different ways and are extremely popular. As can be seen in Juzo Itami's fascinating and seminal film *Tampopo*, the stock, which is made from bones and vegetables and flavored with soy sauce, is very important. The noodles are served in a bowl of stock, usually with slices of roast pork, **shinachiku**, and **kamaboko**. The usual seasoning is a sprinkling of black pepper. Itinerant vendors of *rāmen* ply the streets, usually late at night, announcing themselves with the raucous sound of the *charumera*, a shawm or reed instrument whose name derives from Portuguese *charamela*, but which came to Japan from China and sets a Chinese tone. One of the more terrifying experiences of

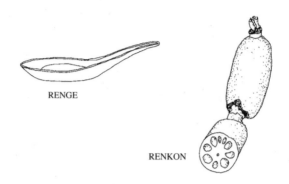

RENGE

RENKON

Japan is to be woken up in the early hours of the morning by this soul-piercing cacophany.

ramune ラムネ lemonade. The bottle of this old-fashioned lemonade is sealed by means of a glass marble inside. The pressure of the CO_2 gas in the lemonade holds the marble in place until the bottle is forced open, usually with a special "key."

renge れんげ 蓮華 china spoon. The full name is **chirirenge**. It has been used in Japan since the Heian period (794–1185), but mostly for Chinese food, especially soups.

rengesō れんげそう 蓮華草 milk vetch *Astragalus sinicus*. The stalks of this wild plant attain between 10 and 25 cm. The buds and young leaves are made into **aemono** and **o-hitashi**, and the flowers are used for tempura.

renkon れんこん 蓮根 lotus root *Nelumbo nucifera*. Actually a rhizome, not a root, it is a very versatile vegetable with a pleasantly crisp texture. It should be boiled in water with a few drops of vinegar in a stainless or enamel pan to keep its white color. It is used in **nimono**, **sunomono**, and tempura. *Karashi renkon*, in which the holes are filled with mustard, is very good as tempura and **kushiage**.

robatayaki ろばたやき 炉辺焼き、 炉端焼き a kind of grilled food. In front of the cook there is a grill, in front of which there is a large counter display of all the different things available for grilling. The customer sits in front of this and tells the cook what he wants. When an order is ready, the cook passes it over the counter to the customer on a long-handled instrument like a bread peel. Beer and saké flow.

ryokutō りょくとう 緑豆 mung bean, green gram *Vigna radiata*. Mainly used in Japan for the production of **mame moyashi**.

ryōri りょうり 料理 1. cookery, cuisine, a style of cooking. 2. a dish or kind of food.

ryōtei りょうてい 料亭 high-class restaurant of Japanese cuisine in which the customers are served in private Japanese-style rooms. The menu is decided by the chef and the food is exquisite if not abundant. Extremely expensive.

—S—

saba さば 鯖、 鮐 chub mackerel, Pacific mackerel *Scomber japonicus* (ma-saba). This handsome fish with a blue-green back and dark markings attains a length of 50 cm or so and a weight of up to 1.8 kg and is best in the autumn, when its fat increases from its normal 4% to 15%. Being such an oily fish, it is good grilled and very good cooked with miso as *saba no misoni*. It is also good in **sunomono**, but cooking methods using oil, such as **kara-age** or tempura, should be avoided. Some people find mackerel indigestible.

sabazushi さばずし 鯖鮨、 鯖鮨 mackerel sushi. A general term for *bōzushi* and **sugatazushi** as well as **nigirizushi** of mackerel. 1. The *saba no bōzushi* 鯖の棒鮨 of Kyoto is the principal type. Long thin strips of transparent **konbu** that have been simmered in sweet vinegar for a long time and long fillets of mackerel prepared with salt and vinegar are pressed onto sushi rice to form a rectangular baton, which is wrapped in bamboo leaves.

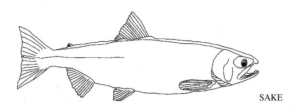

SAKE

To eat, it is unwrapped and cut into 2-cm slices. It mainly differs from the **battera** of Osaka in being shaped with a **makisu**, not pressed in a box. 2. The *saba no sugatazushi* 鯖の姿鮨 of Kochi Prefecture, in which the fish is stuffed so that the original shape is maintained.

saibashi さいばし 菜箸 1. kitchen chopsticks. They are usually made of bamboo and often come in a set of large, medium, and small, which is nevertheless rather longer than table chopsticks. For arranging food on vessels, professionals use sharply pointed steel chopsticks with wooden handles. 2. serving chopsticks. These are a feature of **kaiseki ryōri 2**.

sakana 1. さかな 肴 food eaten with saké and other alcoholic drinks. It is often referred to as *sake no sakan*a, to distinguish it from **sakana 2**. There is no set list of food items, which are also called *o-tsumami*, *tsumami*, and **tsumamimono**.

sakana 2. さかな 魚 fish. An important constituent of the traditional Japanese diet and the main source of animal protein. When the fish is absolutely fresh, the preferred method of serving is as sashimi. Next come the various methods of grilling and frying. Fish that is not as fresh as it might be can be served as **sunomono** or **nimono**.

sakazuki さかずき 杯、盃 saké cup. Usually a small china vessel containing hardly more than a mouthful. *See also* **choko**.

saké 1. さけ 酒 rice wine. Wine is something of a misnomer since saké is produced by brewing. There is an enormous range of flavor and quality, and the taste ranges from very dry to fairly sweet. The alcohol content is about 16%. Saké may be served warmed or chilled. Drinking it warmed seems somehow more convivial, but connoisseurs drinking high-quality saké will have it chilled or at room temperature. Also called **nihonshu**. *See also* Appendix 7.

sake 2. さけ　鮭　chum salmon, dog salmon *Oncorhyncus keta*. This is the salmon of the northern rivers and waters of Japan. Also called *shirozake*, and in the speech of Tokyo *shake*. It has a beautiful silvery dark blue back and silvery white belly, grows up to 1 m in length, though a usual size would be 70 cm with a weight of 3 kg. From September to January salmon return to the river of their birth for spawning, swimming upstream about 14 km in a day, and are at their best for eating in October. The season for the salmon from the high seas, which is preferred for food, is from the beginning of May to the end of June. Fresh salmon, whether as sashimi or grilled or sautéed, is not part of traditional Japanese cuisine, and a large part of the catch is salted as *shiozake*. It is then grilled (a breakfast favorite), prepared as **namasu** (especially the head cartilage), used in **nabemono**, or steamed with saké as *sakamushi*. Nowadays fresh salmon is used for sushi or sautéed in butter. The roe is considered a great delicacy and is salted either as **sujiko** or **ikura**.

sakekasu さけかす　酒粕　saké lees. The remains of the rice filtered out when saké has brewed contain about 8% alcohol. This product is used for making soup, instant **amazake**, and certain pickles, for which *see also* **tsukemono**.

sakura さくら　桜　cherry *Prunus* spp., e.g. *Jamasakura, lannesiana, maximowiczii*. 1. The salt-pickled flowers are used for a "tea" served at celebrations such as weddings. The leaves are also pickled in salt and used to wrap a kind of **mochi** called *sakuramochi*. 2. At a **soba** shop *sakura* refers to a small serving.

sakura ebi さくらえび　桜海老　sakura shrimp *Sergestes lucens*. *See also* **ebi**.

SANMA

sakuranbo さくらんぼ　桜ん坊、　桜桃　cherry (fruit). Several varieties are grown as a dessert fruit in Japan, but compared with those imported from the US and New Zealand, the local product is extremely expensive. *Sakuranbō* is the colloquial pronunciation.

sakura niku さくらにく　桜肉　horse meat. Literally the Japanese word means cherry meat.

same さめ　鮫　sharks Orders Lamniformes and Squaliformes. Shark has a limited appeal as food, not least because the dead flesh soon develops an ammoniac smell. For this reason, it is best prepared as **sunomono** or used in **kamaboko**. Miyoshi, in Hiroshima Prefecture, is famous for its *wani sashimi*. Though *wani* normally means crocodile in Japanese, in this case it refers to sharks of the Family Odontaspididae.

sanbaizu さんばいず　三杯酢　vinegar mixture containing soy sauce and **mirin** (or sugar), often diluted with **dashi**. It is used with vegetables and fish and is good as a dressing for crab.

sanma さんま　秋刀魚　Pacific saury *Cololabis saira*. This long, thin fish of the northern waters grows to a length of 35 cm and is caught in vast quantities in the autumn, arriving in the north of Hokkaido on sea currents from North America at the end of August, and reaching northern Honshu in September and October. Though very oily, being cheap, it is popular in home cooking, especially as **shioyaki** and sometimes **teppanyaki**. It is also eaten as sashimi, **sunomono**, and **sugatazushi**.

sanmaioroshi さんまいおろし　三枚卸し　filleting of fish. The expression, above all a fishmonger's term, means dividing into three, i.e., the two fillets and the head-backbone-tail, which will always be given to the customer unless rejected.

SANSHŌ

sansai 山菜 mountain vegetable. There used to be a clear distinction between *sansai* and **yasai** (cultivated vegetables) but nowadays this is not so clear, since some *sansai*, such as **warabi**, are cultivated, and some *yasai*, such as **mitsuba**, **seri**, and **fuki**, also grow wild. *Sansai* convey a strong sense of spring and are a great favorite of vegetarians, often featuring in the menus of **shōjin ryōri**. For a list of the main *sansai* plants *see also* Appendix 9. The seven herbs of spring and autumn, though mostly picked from the wild, are not generally included in the category of *sansai*, perhaps because they are regarded as medicine rather than food. *See also* **nanakusagayu**.

sansai ryōri さんさいりょうり 山菜料理 cooking with wild herbs and vegetables. Many of these herbs and vegetables need preliminary preparation, such as blanching, to remove bitterness. After this, they are usually prepared as tempura, soup, **o-hitashi**, **aemono**, or **nimono**. *See also* Appendix 9.

sanshō さんしょう 山椒 Japanese pepper *Zanthoxylum piperitum*. The seedpods of the Japanese prickly ash are ground and used as pepper, above all in the seven-spice mixture **shichimi tōgarashi**. These pods are aromatic rather than hot and have a slightly numbing after-effect on the tongue, very similar to that of the closely related Szechwan pepper, *Zanthoxylum bungeanum* (or *Zanthoxylum bungei* or *Zanthoxylum simulans*). (Note: *Fagara* is no longer used as the genus name for any of the prickly ashes.) *Sanshō* is usually bought ground, since it keeps its aroma pretty well. It is

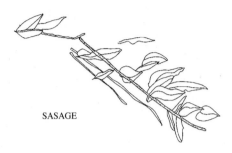

SASAGE

mostly used with grilled eel and chicken to counteract the flavor and smell of fat. Sprigs of **kinome** (the young leaves of *sanshō*) provide a highly aromatic addition to many dishes, whether as an edible garnish or as herbal ingredient, chopped, brayed, or made into a paste. These little leaves are used to good effect in **suimono**, **aemono**, **yakimono**, and **tsukemono**. Their aroma, which is in the area of mint and basil with a touch of licorice, is brought out with gentle beating. The seeds of *sanshō*, which are very bitter, are not used, being removed from the pods and discarded. A pickle is made of the berries.

sara さら 皿 dish, plate. Different kinds of food need different types of dishes, and the different seasons require different designs. Restaurants and even families are likely to have a large collection of dishes.

sarashi negi さらしねぎ 晒し葱 finely sliced **negi** refreshed in chilled water. It is added to the **ponzu** dip for **mizutaki**.

sasa ささ 笹 bamboo grass *Sasa* spp. *See also* **nemagaritake**.

sasage ささげ 大角豆 cowpea, black-eyed pea *Vigna unguiculata*. These long, thin-podded beans are used mainly for their seeds, which can be white, red, yellow, or black, and are highly nutritious, being a good source of protein. The immature beans are used as a vegetable, whereas the mature ones are mostly used as an alternative to **azuki** beans. They are used for making **an**, and the red ones can be used instead of *azuki* in **sekihan**.

SASARA

sasamaki ささまき 笹巻き a kind of sushi made from **ayu**, **aji**, **kohada**, or other fish prepared with salt and vinegar and then wrapped up in the leaves of **sasa**, a kind of bamboo. It is unwrapped before being eaten.

sasami ささみ 笹身 the fillet from the breast of chicken that is sold separately.

sasara ささら 簓 strong brush made of long, thin slivers of bamboo, used for cleaning pots, graters, and other cooking utensils.

sashimi さしみ 刺身 raw fish, shellfish, and crustaceans. A cardinal principle of Japanese cuisine is that any seafood fresh enough to be eaten raw, should be served raw. As sashimi implies slicing, raw oysters are not sashimi but raw slices of scallop are. Preparing sashimi is the preserve of professionals such as sushi chefs, since experience and skill are essential, not least in the sharpening and care of the high-quality knives used. This is especially true of **ikizukuri**, in which the fish is sliced while still alive and replaced on the skeleton to serve in a decorative manner. For home eating, sashimi is usually bought prepared by the fishmonger. It is eaten at the beginning of the meal with a dip of soy sauce and grated **wasabi**, often with the addition of **benitade**. Octopus, when eaten as sashimi, is normally boiled first, but squid is eaten raw. Chicken, beef, horse meat, whale, and **namasu** are also served as sashimi. Sashimi is one kind of **namasu**.

satō さとう 砂糖 sugar. Almost all Japanese sugar is made from sugar cane, *satō kibi* さとうきび 砂糖黍 *Saccharum offici-*

SATOIMO

narum, though a small amount of very high-grade sugar is made from Chinese sugar cane, *chikusha* ちくしゃ 竹蔗 *Saccharum sinense*, for which *see also* **wasanbon** and Appendix 17. Pure white sugar is the norm and is available as granulated, caster, cube, and crystal (candy) sugar. Brown sugar (*kurozatō* くろざとう 黒砂糖) is traditionally sold in rough lumps, and there is a light brown sugar called *san on tō* さんおんとう 三温糖. Syrups from both white and brown sugar are also available. Sugar is used as an all-purpose sweetener and in most prepared foods as a flavoring.

satoimo さといも 里芋 taro, dasheen *Colocasia esculenta*. Cooked by long simmering, these little potato-like corms have a waxy, almost glutinous texture and high sugar content. After simmering, they are often simply served peeled, with salt or soy sauce, a dish known as *kinukatsugi*. They are also prepared in various ways as **nimono**.

satsuma-age さつまあげ 薩摩揚げ another name for **age-kamaboko**.

satsumaimo さつまいも 薩摩芋 sweet potato *Ipomoea batatas*. This South American tuber came to Miyakojima, one of the southernmost Ryukyu Islands, in 1597, and subsequently spread throughout Satsuma (southern Kyushu) in the seventeenth century. Its sweetness makes it a popular snack, especially with children, who like to buy it from the itinerant vendors who bake it in hot pebbles (**ishiyaki imo**) as they wheel their cart (or drive their

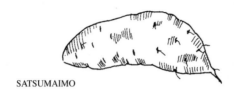

SATSUMAIMO

van) around. At home *satsumaimo* is normally steamed. It is also candied as a confection and as a purée has extensive use in bakery and confectionary.

satsumajiru さつまじる　薩摩汁　hearty soup from southern Kyushu (Satsuma) containing chicken on the bone with lots of vegetables and flavored with miso. Local variations have spread throughout Japan.

sawagani さわがに　沢蟹　river crab *Geothelphusa dehaani*. This very small crab dwells in very clear-watered streams. It is sold live in markets and is usually cooked as **kara-age**. It must be well cooked to avoid parasite (distoma) infection.

sawara さわら　鰆　Spanish mackerel *Scomberomorus niphonius*. One of the larger mackerels (Family Scombridae), growing up to 1 m in length, prevalent in the Inland Sea. Considered to make first-rate eating, it is tastiest in the winter, when its fat increases, but is mostly caught from April to June when it enters the harbors of the Inland Sea for spawning. It should be avoided as sashimi because of parasites, and is best as **shioyaki** or teriyaki.

sayaendō さやえんどう　莢豌豆　edible podded pea, mangetout pea, sugar pea, snow pea *Pisum sativum* var. *sativum*. The young pods of this beautiful green pea are eaten before the peas have fully formed. Once available only in spring, it is nowadays available year-round. It makes a delicious, crunchy addition to many dishes, especially **suimono**, **aemono**, and **o-hitashi**. It is also used in **nimono** and **agemono** and is really good in **itamemono**.

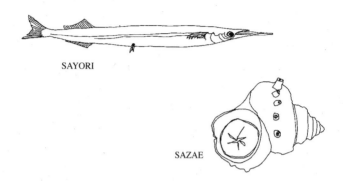

SAYORI

SAZAE

sayaingen さやいんげん 莢隠元 young kidney bean, snap bean, asparagus bean *Phaseolus vulgaris*. Once available only in summer, these beans are now cultivated year-round and freeze well. They add a colorful touch to many different dishes and go particularly well in **aemono**, **agemono**, **itamemono**, and **nimono**.

sayamame さやまめ 莢豆 *See* **edamame**.

sayori さより 細魚、針魚 halfbeak *Hyporhamphus sajori*. Similar to the gar, this small, long-bodied fish has a very short upper jaw. It is a lean fish that can attain a length of 40 cm. Its best season is from spring to autumn. It should be cleaned very thoroughly and can be served as sashimi, tempura, **shioyaki**, or **sunomono**.

sazae さざえ 栄螺、拳螺 turbo, top-shell *Batillus cornutus*. This gastropod, about 10 cm high and 8 cm around, may be eaten as sashimi, but the favorite way of dealing with it is grilled in the shell over a direct flame (**tsuboyaki**) and then served cold with a toothpick to extract it from the shell. At the far end of the muscle is the dark green **wata** (intestines and reproductive gland), which is also eaten. *Sazae* is in season from spring to summer and is very tasty.

seirō, seiro せいろう、 せいろ 蒸龍 steamer of the traditional kind, as distinct from the modern **mushiki**. Two types of *seirō* are in use. One is the traditional Japanese type, known as *wa seirō* or

KAKU SEIRŌ

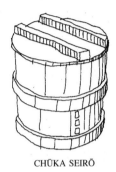

CHŪKA SEIRŌ

kaku seirō, a square framework made of wood. A square board with one or more holes is placed on top of a pot of boiling water, and on top of that is a square frame, fitted with crosspieces on which a bamboo mat is set. The food to be steamed is placed on top of this, and the square wooden lid put in place. The other traditional steamer is the Chinese type, *chūka seirō*, circular and made of bamboo. It works the same way as the Japanese type, but does not have a board as base. In both cases, several layers can be placed on top of each other. The Japanese wooden type is considerably more expensive than the Chinese bamboo type.

seiyōwasabi せいようわさび　西洋山葵 horseradish *Armoracia rusticana*. *See also* **wasabi daikon**.

sekihan せきはん　赤飯 celebratory rice dish made from glutinous rice and some non-glutinous rice, steamed with **azuki** or **sasage** beans. It is also called **o-kowa**.

senbei せんべい　煎餅 rice cracker, biscuit. Coming within the general category of **higashi**, the salty ones are made from rice flour, the sweet ones from wheat flour with eggs, sugar, and even miso. Sweetened soy sauce is often brushed on while they are being grilled. Lacking fat, they go stale very quickly.

SERI

sencha せんちゃ　煎茶　good-quality green tea. *See also* Appendix 12.

sengiri せんぎり　千切り、繊切り　shredded, sliced into shreds or thin strips, julienne. The shredded cabbage served with **tonkatsu** is an example.

senmaizuke せんまいづけ　千枚漬け　a famous Kyoto pickle of **kabu**. The variety used is the large *shōgoin* 聖護院, which can weigh up to 4 kg. It is sliced thinly and salt-pickled with **konbu**, sugar or **mirin**, and chili pepper for up to a month, during which its special flavor develops. It is rich in **umami**, for which *see also* Appendix 14.

seri せり　芹　water dropwort *Oenanthe javanica*. *Seri* grows along streams and marshes and is best from autumn to spring, although it is picked year-round. It makes an excellent vegetable for sukiyaki. It is also added to soups and salads and goes well with chicken. In appearance it is very similar to **mitsuba**, coriander, or celery leaves. Some consider the flavor to be like that of parsley, others like that of carrot. *See also* **nanakusagayu**, **sansai**, and **sansai ryōri**.

shabu shabu しゃぶしゃぶ　**nabemono** featuring thin slices of beef with vegetables. The name is onomatopoeic for the sound made when the beef is dipped in the stock. It is a favorite winter dish supposedly derived from the Mongolian hotpot of Chinese cookery and is sometimes cooked in a Chinese-style "fire pot," *fuoguo-*

SHAKO

zu ホーゴーズ　火鍋子, pronounced *hōgōzu*, from the Chinese *huoguozi*, also called *hōkōtsu* ホーコーツ.

shagō しゃごう　*See* **shako 1**.

shako 1. しゃこ、しゃこがい　硨磲貝　giant clam *Tridaena gigas*. This huge clam, with a shell 1 m high, is found in the coral reefs to the southwest of the Ogasawara Islands and is eaten in Okinawa. The flesh nearest the shell is the tastiest and the adductor muscle is very good dried and added to soups or used in other ways.

shako 2. しゃこ　蝦蛄、青竜蝦　mantis shrimp, squilla *Oratosquilla oratoria*. The English name indicates that this creature is the marine counterpart of the praying mantis insect. Growing to a length of 15 cm, it lives in its own hole in shallow coastal waters all around Japan. When boiled and removed from the shell, a professional task, it has a purplish skin and whitish flesh. It is most used as a topping for **nigirizushi**, but can also be used for tempura. It is particularly good when with roe.

shamisengai しゃみせんがい　三味線貝　tongue clam, lamp shell *Lingula jaspidea*. This brachiopod, strictly speaking not a shellfish, belongs to the oldest living genus of animals, almost unchanged for 500,000,000 years. A greenish color, about 3 cm long with a peduncle about 5 cm long, it is harvested in quantity from the Ariake Sea in northwestern Kyushu. It tastes peculiar rather than delicious and some people come out in a rash when they eat

SHAMISENGAI

it. Eleven species of *Lingula*, some quite large, live in Japanese waters, but after surviving since the Cambrian period, are now being wiped out by pollution.

shibazuke しばづけ　柴漬け　salt-pickled eggplant. A justly famous Kyoto pickle of eggplant with **myōga**, red **shiso**, and sometimes a little chili pepper.

shichimi tōgarashi しちみとうがらし　七味唐辛子　seven-spice chili mix. The name literally means seven-flavor chili. In the Tokyo area it is called *nanairo tōgarashi*, seven-color chili. Chili powder without any admixture is called *ichimi tōgarashi*, one-flavor chili. *Shichimi* is chili with (at least) six additions. The formula is flexible and there are shops that will make a mix according to the customer's wishes. However, there are two commercially well-established formulae: the Yagenbori *shichimi* of Tokyo, containing ground chili, both toasted and dried, with mustard, **sanshō**, black sesame, poppy seeds, hemp (cannabis) seeds, and **chinpi**; and the Kiyomizu *shichimi* of Kyoto, containing chili, **sanshō**, black and white sesame, **aonori**, **shiso**, and hemp seeds. These mixtures are sprinkled on noodles, **nabemono**, and **yakitori**. Usually traditional shakers of wood or bamboo are used. Often simply called *shichimi*.

shichirin しちりん　七厘、七輪　portable brazier for cooking. With the same uses as a **konro**, or stove top, it is made of clay. Charcoal is used for fuel.

SHIITAKE

shiira しいら 鱪、鱰 dolphin fish, dorado *Coryphaena hippurus*.
A long, slim sea fish growing to about 2 m, especially found on
the Japan Sea side of Japan. It is a good source of protein, tastes
best in summer, but is inclined to be watery and is eaten as sashimi
only when really fresh. Cooking with oil is best. The fish is also
salted and dried and in this form is used as a celebratory gift in the
Kochi and Kumamoto areas.

shiitake しいたけ 椎茸 shiitake mushroom *Lentinus edodes*. The
best known of the Japanese fungi, no doubt because it is extensively cultivated and preserved by drying. It has a strong, distinct
flavor, which, though very attractive and popular in Japanese food,
does not on the whole go well with Western dishes, as **maitake**
does. It is named after a tree called *shii*, a kind of chestnut-oak
(*Castanopsis cuspidata*), on the cut logs of which it is cultivated
for spring and autumn crops. It is best bought in the form called
donko 冬菇, in which the caps are well formed but still curled under. Fresh *shiitake* is very good as tempura, in **nabemono**, or just
brushed with oil, lightly salted, and grilled. The dried ones, which
keep almost indefinitely in a well-sealed container, are used for
making stock in **shōjin ryōri**, and after soaking can be used in rice
and noodle dishes and in many other ways.

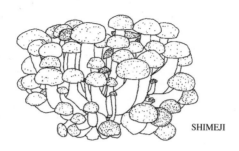

SHIMEJI

shijimi しじみ 蜆 Japanese freshwater clam, corbicula *Astarte polaris*. A rather small clam of 3 cm or less, this is a great favorite in miso soup. These clams grow in the brackish water of lakes and rivers near the sea. They can be freeze-dried in the shell very successfully and are thus very useful in freeze-dried miso soups.

shima しま- 縞- prefix meaning striped. *Shima-aji*, striped jack *Pseudocaranx dentex*, is an example.

shimeji しめじ 湿地、占地 shimeji mushroom *Lyophyllum* spp. Clusters of a very delicately straw-colored cultivated mushroom with a cap of about 1 cm in diameter are often sold in supermarkets as **honshimeji**. Actually, they are *buna shimeji*, an excellent substitute. *See also* **honshimeji**.

shimofuri しもふり 霜降 1. blanching of fish and poultry. The food can either be immersed in boiling water for thirty seconds to a minute, or a large quantity of boiling water can be poured over it. 2. marbled beef.

shin しん- 新- prefix meaning new. *Shinmai* is newly harvested rice, and *shincha* is the new season's tea.

shinachiku しなちく 支那竹 lactic ferment pickle of bamboo shoot. Chinese in origin, this brownish pickle is made by slicing bamboo shoot thinly, steaming it, salting it, allowing a lactic ferment to develop, and finally drying it in the sun. It is one of the ingredients of **rāmen** and is also called *menma* メンマ 麺媽.

shinko 1. しんこ　新香　pickles not intended to be stored, and also a general term for pickles.

shinko 2. しんこ　新粉　non-glutinous rice flour. Polished rice is washed and drained, ground into a fine flour while still damp, and then dried. The top grade, which is very fine, is called *jōshin-ko* 上糝粉、 上新粉 and is particularly used for making **dango** and various **wagashi**.

shio しお　塩　salt. All salt produced in Japan comes from sea water, and most table salt is locally produced. *See also* Appendix 8.

shiokara しおから　塩辛　salt-cured preserve of fish, mollusks, and their entrails. After pickling in salt, the protein of the seafood undergoes a process of maturation, resulting in particularly tasty combinations of amino acids. The most popular *shiokara* is that of squid; the most high class, the entrails of the sea slug (**konowata**). *See also* Appendix 14.

shioyaki しおやき　塩焼き　salt-grilling. A simple but excellent method of cooking fish.

shiozuke しおづけ　塩漬け　salt pickle. The commonest form of pickling vegetables, often a light, brief process done for flavor rather than preservation.

shira ae しらあえ　白和え　a cooked salad (**aemono**) of which the dressing (**koromo**) is made of tofu.

shirako しらこ　白子　soft roe, milt. The sperm-filled reproductive gland of male fish. The milt of **tara** (cod), **ankō** (angler fish), and **fugu** (puffer) is regarded as especially tasty and is used in soups, **nabemono**, and **aemono**.

shirasu[boshi] しらす[ぼし]　白子[干し]　*See* **chirimenjako**.

shirataki しらたき　白滝　thin noodles of **konnyaku**. A standard ingredient of sukiyaki, it is a little thinner and softer than *ito konnyaku*. *See also* **konnyaku**.

shiratamako しらたまこ　白玉粉　glutinous rice-flour granules. The process of manufacture is similar to that of **shinko 2**, except

SHIROURI

that the end product takes the form of large granules, which are used in cooking for thickening and in **wagashi** confectionary.

shirauo しらうお　白魚　whitebait, Japanese icefish *Salangichthys microdon*. A harbor fish found throughout Japan, it can reach a length of 10 cm. Live, it is practically transparent, but dead, it becomes opaque white. It makes excellent tempura and can be added to **chawan mushi** and **chirinabe**, and sometimes, out of confusion with **shirouo**, is used for **odorigui**, when it is swallowed alive.

shiroan しろあん　白餡　*See* **an**.

shiromiso しろみそ　白味噌　white miso. *See also* Appendix 6.

shiromizakana しろみざかな　白身魚　white-fleshed fish. The term is used to exclude such fish as tuna or sardines, which have extensive *chiai* 血合, flesh richly colored with blood. **Hirame**, **isaki**, **karei**, **kochi**, **tai**, and **tara** are examples. White-fleshed fish is very popular cooked as **furai**.

shirouo しろうお　素魚　ice goby *Leucopsarion petersi*. A scale-less coastal fish growing to a length of 8 cm. When alive, the fish is very tasty, but dead, it quickly deteriorates. This has given rise to the unusual method of eating, originating in Fukuoka, known as **odorigui**, in which the fish is swallowed alive.

shirouri しろうり　白瓜、越瓜　Oriental pickling melon. This melon has been cultivated in Japan at least since the tenth century. It usually has a weight of from 3 to 5 kg and is mainly used for making a pickle called **narazuke**. *See also* **tsukemono**.

SHISO

SHISONOMI

shiru しる 汁 soup. The word can have a variety of connotations, including juice, liquid, and gravy.

shiruko しるこ 汁粉 sweet soup made from the **an** of **azuki** beans with **mochi** or **dango** of **shiratamako** added. If the *an* is not sieved, the soup is called **zenzai**.

shishamo ししゃも 柳葉魚 Japanese capelin, shishamo smelt *Spirinchus lanceolatus*. Although this 15-cm fish is caught in the mouths of rivers in southern Hokkaido in autumn, when it is carrying roe and at its tastiest, most of the *shishamo* consumed in Japan is imported. It is mildly salt-dried and is delicious grilled or fried.

shishitō 獅子唐 *See* **shishitōgarashi**.

shishitōgarashi ししとうがらし 獅子唐辛子 sweet green pepper *Capsicum annuum* var. *angulosum*. Although the flavor of this pepper is even milder than that of the closely related **pīman**, it looks remarkably like a hot green chili. It is usually grilled on a skewer, often between pieces of chicken, with which it goes well. It can also be stir-fried and is good as tempura.

shiso しそ 紫蘇 perilla, beefsteak plant *Perilla frutescens* var. *crispa*. This largish (8 x 5 cm) leaf, of which there are two kinds, green and red, has many uses. The red leaves (**akajiso**) are used mostly to give their color to pickles, especially **umeboshi**. Green shiso (**aojiso**) has many uses at table. *Shiso* is a member of the

mint family, and the green leaves have a hint of basil and spear-
mint, which can be particularly appreciated when the leaf is finely chopped and added to hot rice. It is served with sashimi (and
should be eaten with it), made into tempura, and used in various
ways to garnish sushi. The buds are made into a strong-flavored
condiment, and the very young buds on the stalk are made into
tempura.

shisonomi しそのみ　紫蘇の実　the very young buds of **shiso**. They
make good tempura on the stalk, make an attractive garnish, and
are used in **aemono** and **suimono**.

shitabirame　したびらめ　舌鮃、　舌平目　sole Order Pleuronec-
tiformes suborder Soleoidei. Among these numerous kinds of flatfish, the best are considered to be *kuroushinoshita* (*Paraplagusia
japonica*) at 35 cm, *akashitabirame* (*Cynoglossus joyneri*) at 24
cm, and *setoushinoshita* (*Pseudaesopia japonica*) at 15 cm. Soles
are not so much part of the Japanese cuisine as they are of the
Western, but they are excellent grilled as **shioyaki**, and after skin-
ning they may be simmered as **nimono** or used for sushi, tempura,
or **furai**.

shōchū しょうちゅう　焼酎　distilled spirits. With a superficial simi-
larity to vodka, this drink may be made from sweet potato, common
potato, rice, barley, buckwheat, millet, or maize with sugar syrup.
Legally the alcohol content should not exceed 36% but sometimes
reaches up to 45%. *Shōchū* may be drunk "on the rocks" but is
normally mixed with hot water (*yuwari* 湯割り), usually in equal
parts (*gōgōwari*), or with slightly more hot water (*rokuyonwari*).
There is also a popular drink in which *shōchū* is mixed with soda
water and a little syrup of various flavors, and served with ice and
lemon. This is the *shōchū* highball called *chūhai*.

shōga　しょうが　生姜、　生薑、　薑　ginger *Zingiber officinale*.
Fresh ginger has many uses, for both the fresh rhizome and the
leaf-bearing shoot (**hajikami**). The very young rhizome is pickled in vinegar, as is the shoot. These are especially used with fish

to mask the smell, as is grated fresh ginger and its juice. Grated ginger is also added to the dip for tempura. Thinly sliced pickled ginger (**gari**) is always served lavishly with sushi as a digestive condiment. *Beni shōga* 紅生姜 is sliced ginger that has turned red as a result of first being pickled in salt, then in vinegar. The resultant *beni shōga* acquires a more vivid color if it is kept in **ume** vinegar with red **shiso** leaves. It is also artificially colored with garish effect.

shōjin ryōri しょうじんりょうり　精進料理　the most widespread system of Zen Buddhist vegetarianism. *See also* Appendix 15.

shokuji しょくじ　食事　meal. The Japanese norm is three meals a day, at which there should be some staple such as rice (or bread) to qualify. A proper meal would also have soup and pickles. Drinking while eating lots of different foods (without rice) does not constitute a meal, so men who spend the evening drinking with friends or colleagues may well not have an evening meal, even though they have had a lot to eat. They will probably have **o-cha-zuke** when they get home.

shottsuru しょっつる　塩汁、醢汁　*See* **uoshōyu**.

shōyu しょうゆ　醤油　soy sauce. The essential, basic flavorer of Japanese food, made from soybeans, wheat, and salt. *Shōyu* has a strong savory aroma and is quite salty (from 15 to 20%). There is no substitute for the Japanese product, which is usually available at table as well as being much used in the kitchen. There are several varieties and many different qualities, to which price is a reliable guide. At table *koikuchi shōyu* (heavy soy sauce) is used, whereas in cooking, *usukuchi shōyu* (light soy sauce) is often used. Heavy soy sauce is less salty than light and since light soy sauce is not always available abroad, it does no great harm to use heavy soy sauce instead. *See also* Appendix 10.

shūmai シューマイ　焼売　Chinese dumpling (dim sum) that, along with **gyōza**, has become a familiar part of Japanese food life. Finely ground pork, or sometimes shrimp or even beef, seasoned

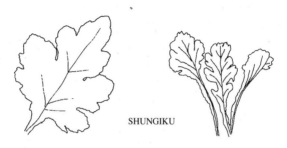

SHUNGIKU

with onion, ginger, pepper, salt, and soy sauce, is placed in cups of thin wheat pastry and steamed. Often found in **bentō**.

shun しゅん 旬 the best season for any fish, mollusk, vegetable, or fruit.

shungiku しゅんぎく 春菊 garland chrysanthemum *Chrysanthemum coronarium*. The leaves of *shungiku*, which means spring chrysanthemum, have a strong, distinct flavor and are used as a vegetable. The autumn crop should correctly be called *kikuna* (vegetable chrysanthemum). Chrysanthemum leaves are especially popular in **nabemono** but are also much used in **aemono** and **o-hitashi**.

soba そば 蕎麦 buckwheat *Fagopyrum esculentum*. 1. an herbaceous plant cultivated for its pyramidal seeds. It takes two to three months to grow, with crops in summer and autumn, but production in Japan has long been in decline and a very high proportion is now imported. Buckwheat is useful because it grows in cold mountainous regions where rice, barley, and wheat cannot grow, and also is extremely nutritious, being rich in protein, rutin, and vitamins E and C. The husk, which is particularly tough, is removed and used as a filling for pillows. The seeds are ground into flour of various grades, much of which is made into noodles. The seeds are also parboiled and cooked with rice, and are also used for making beer, vodka, and **shōchū**. The honey of bees that frequent fields of buckwheat is very good indeed. 2. buckwheat noodles. A wide variety of noodles is made from buckwheat flour, usually with some wheat flour and sometimes powdered green tea added. For *zarusoba* ざるそば　笊蕎麦 the noodles are boiled and served cold on a draining mat. For **wankosoba** わんこそば 椀子蕎麦, a specialty of Iwate Prefecture, mouthfuls of boiled noodles are served in a succession of bowls with a dipping broth and a wide variety of accompaniments to add flavor. The simplest way of serving *soba* is *kake* かけ　掛け, in a good broth with some chili and **sarashi negi** sprinkled on top. *See also* **rāmen** and **chūkasoba**.

sobako そばこ　蕎麦扮 buckwheat flour. There are several grades, milled from both the polished and unpolished grain. For use, the flour is mixed with wheat flour in appropriate proportions.

soboro そぼろ crumble topping for which minced chicken or meat; shredded, boiled shrimp and fish; and scrambled egg are lightly parched, seasoning being optional. Each ingredient is arranged in a separate field to form a colorful pattern, usually on top of rice in a **bentō** or **donburi**.

sōmen そうめん　素麺 thin wheat noodles. Usually served cold as a refreshing summer dish, these are dried noodles, which since they must still be quite firm after cooking, are boiled just briefly and then immediately refreshed in cold water. They are served with a chilled dipping broth and **sarashi negi**. *See also* **hiyamugi**.

soramame そらまめ　蚕豆、空豆 broad bean, fava bean *Vicia faba*. These beans have been cultivated in Japan since the eighth century. They are picked in May and June and, when boiled in salted water and served plain, make a very good accompaniment to summer drinks, especially beer. They are also used as an ingredient of **nimono** and can be added to soup as a puree. The pods are large, having a diameter of about 3 cm.

sōsu ソース *See* **usutā sōsu**.

sōzai そうざい　惣菜、総菜 side dish. Any of the dishes accompanying rice, miso soup, and pickles. Often preceded by the honorific *o-*. Also called **o-kazu**.

su す 酢 vinegar. A variety of vinegars is made in Japan, all of them fermented from rice and fairly mild in flavor, having about 4.2% acidity. Non-rice vinegars do not make suitable substitutes. Naturally brewed vinegar is expensive but very good. Best of all is *genmai mochigome su*, the hard-to-come-by vinegar made from unpolished glutinous rice.

sudachi すだち 酢橘、 酸橘 sharp (acidic) citrus fruit *Citrus sudachi*. Smaller than its close relative the **yuzu**, it has the same pale-yellow color when ripe. Unlike the *yuzu*, it is used, usually while still green (in summer and autumn), for its sharp juice and fragrant zest. It goes very well with **matsutake**.

sugaki すがき 酢牡蠣 oysters in vinegar. The **sunomono** of raw oysters, which should be added to the vinegar, in the form of **ponzu** or **nihaizu**, just before eating. Grated ginger makes a good addition. Vinegar helps to overcome the nauseating smell of raw oysters, but does not necessarily make them safer to eat.

sugatazushi すがたずし 姿鮨 sushi in which the shape of the fish is retained. Usually **ayu** (sweetfish), **tai** (sea bream), or **saba** (mackerel) is gutted and boned from the belly, the head remaining intact. After preparation with salt and vinegar, the fish is stuffed with rice, sliced, and served in its original shape.

sugukina すぐきな 酸茎菜 a kind of turnip *Brassica campestris* var. *neosuguki*. The famous Kyoto pickle *suguki* is a salt pickle of this vegetable with its leaves, matured as a natural lactic ferment under pressure from the weight of stones.

suihanki すいはんき 炊飯器 automatic rice cooker. Both electric and gas models are available, and it is said that the gas type more nearly reproduces the cooking process of the traditional **kama**. The latest electric models, with memory chips and fuzzy and "neuro" logic, are very sophisticated pieces of equipment.

suika すいか 西瓜 watermelon *Citrullus lanatus*. Popular as a summer fruit, it is often served with a little salt for dessert.

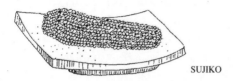

SUJIKO

suikuchi すいくち 吸い口 an ingredient, the fragrance of which strikes the nose when the lid is lifted from a bowl of food or soup, especially **suimono**. It may be **yuzu**, **sanshō**, **wasabi**, ginger, or anything else with sufficient fragrance.

suimono すいもの 吸い物 clear soup. A very elegant kind of consommé, it should be made from the best stock (*ichiban dashi*). Three solid ingredients (**wandane**, **wanzuma**, and **suikuchi**) are added for flavor, color, and aroma, e.g., shrimp with slices of mushroom and a sliver of **yuzu** peel. The soup should be served in a lidded bowl, so that when the lid is removed at table, the full strength of the aroma will regale the diner. The prefix *o-* 御- (*o-suimono* 御吸い物) is a polite addition.

suizenji nori すいぜんじのり 水前寺海苔 Suizenji nori *Aphanothece sacra*. A blue-green freshwater alga, it is cultivated on the pebbly bottoms of clear-flowing streams near Kurume and Amagi in northern Kyushu. When harvested, it is spread on unglazed tiles and dried into sheets. Alternatively, it can be packed in sweetened brine until use, e.g., in soups or **sunomono**. It is also served as an accompaniment for sashimi, and being rare and expensive, it is considered a **chinmi**.

sujiko すじこ 筋子 salmon eggs (roe, red caviar) in the sac. Preserved with salt, the eggs may be eaten as they are or pickled with saké lees (as *kasuzuke*, for which *see also* **tsukemono**), but it is usual to free the eggs from the sac and use them as **ikura**.

sukesōdara すけそうだら 助惣鱈、助宗鱈 *See* **suketōdara**.

suketōdara すけとうだら　介党鱈　Alaska pollack, walleye pollack *Theragra chalcogramma*. Also called **mentai**, it is a smallish kind of cod, growing to a length of about 60 cm. It likes the cold northern waters and is at its best in January and February. It is not much eaten raw, but is used in **nabemono** and **nitsuke** and is dried. The roe is very popular preserved with salt and ground chili, being called *karashimentai* からしめんたい　辛子明太. *See also* **mentaiko**.

sukiyaki すきやき　鋤焼き　**nabemono** of beef and vegetables. It is thought to have been concocted in the Meiji era (1868–1912) to encourage the Japanese to eat beef after Emperor Meiji instructed them to do so. Thin slices of fat-marbled beef are cooked in a shallow, cast-iron pan, with various vegetables, including **negi** and **shungiku**, tofu, and **shirataki**. Sugar or **mirin** and soy sauce are liberally added as the cooking medium, and when the various things are cooked, they are dipped in raw egg and eaten. From this bare description the dish does not seem very inviting, but sitting on tatami in the inebriated mood of a party, most people enjoy it greatly. There are specialist restaurants that only serve sukiyaki.

sumashijiru すましじる　澄まし汁、　清まし汁　clear soup, **suimono**. The stock, *sumashijitate* すましじたて　澄まし仕立て, is *ichiban dashi* with salt and soy sauce added. *See also* **dashi**.

sumibiyaki すみびやき　炭火焼き　charcoal grilling. Charcoal is considered the best fuel for grilling and its lack of smoke makes it especially useful indoors. Coffee roasted over charcoal is highly regarded, but why this makes any difference is hard to understand, since there is no direct contact between the flames and the coffee beans, as in grilling. It seems an emotional rather than a logical appeal, in fact, a rip-off.

sumiso すみそ　酢味噌　white miso thinned with vinegar. Mostly used as a dressing (**koromo**) for **aemono**, it is also used in the preparation of freshwater fish.

SURIBACHI   SURIKOGI

sunagimo すなぎも 砂肝 chicken gizzard. It can be used in many kinds of dishes but is best known in **yakitori**.

sunazuri すなずり 砂摩り、腴 **yakitori** parlance for **sunagimo**.

sunomono すのもの 酢の物 salad dressed with vinegar. A typical example would be thinly sliced cucumber dressed with lightly sweetened vinegar. Slices of seafood may be added or may be the principal ingredient. Various vinegars, including **nihaizu** or **sanbaizu**, may be used. **Sunomono** is a basic dish on any menu.

suppon すっぽん 鼈 snapping turtle, soft-shelled turtle *Trionyx sinensis japonicus*. Plentiful in the rivers of western Japan, it is also farmed and imported. When the turtle is fully grown, its carapace is about 13 cm wide and 17 cm long, greenish brown when from the wild and black when farmed. Not only is turtle highly nutritious but the flesh and especially the blood, which is drunk mixed with saké, are thought to be aphrodisiac. *Suppon* makes delicious stock and is therefore good in **suimono**, **nabemono**, and **zōsui**. It is also deep-fried and served as sashimi.

suribachi すりばち 擂り鉢 ribbed mortar. The inside of this pottery mortar is marked in a broad sweeping pattern with a wide fork. Many sizes, from about 8 cm up, are available. The markings on the inside prevent ingredients from slipping around while being brayed, thus making this kind of mortar particularly useful for grinding such things as sesame.

surikogi すりこぎ 擂り粉木 pestle used with **suribachi**. Various woods are used, but the hardest and therefore the best is the wood of prickly ash (**sanshō**).

surimi すりみ 擂り身 fine paste of fish, shellfish, or chicken, made in a **suribachi**. *Surimi* of whitefish or squid is the basis of **kamaboko** and **chikuwa**.

surume するめ 鯣 dried squid. Popular as **tsumamimono**, it is lightly toasted and cut into strips or bought already in strips.

sushi すし 鮨、鮓、寿司 any of various preparations of vinegared rice with raw fish. *See also* Appendix 11.

suzuke すづけ 酢漬け vinegar pickle. *See also* **tsukemono**.

suzuki すずき 鱸 sea bass *Lateolabrax japonicus*. This beautiful, delicious fish is caught particularly in summer, reaching a length of 1 m. It is also farmed. Served as sashimi, it is also good in **nabemono** and **mushimono**.

suzume すずめ 雀 sparrow *Passer montanus*. Most commonly grilled as **yakitori**. The bird is gutted and eaten bones and all with the head, which is crunched whole. The flesh can also be pounded into balls to go into broth.

suzuna すずな 菘 *See* **kabu** and **nanakusagayu**.

suzushiro すずしろ 清白、蘿蔔 *See* **daikon** and **nanakusagayu**.

—T—

tachiuo たちうお 太刀魚 hairtail, cutlass fish *Trichiurus lepturus*. The long, eel-like body of this fish is a beautiful shiny silver color, with the tail ending in a hairlike thread. The head looks rather vicious with sharp teeth. Reaching a length of 1.5 m, it is a good eating fish, being prepared as sashimi, **sunomono**, **yakimono**, and **kara-age**.

tade たで 蓼 water pepper *Polygonum hydropiper*. There are two kinds with quite different uses. The green variety, *yanagitade*, also called *hontade* and *ma-tade*, is an annual herb growing to a height of between 30 and 80 cm and having willow-like leaves 5 to 10 cm

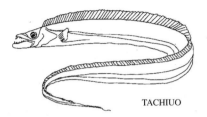

TACHIUO

long. It is mainly used in fish cookery to remove the smell. *Tade su* is a dip served with **ayu** and is made by steeping the pounded leaves or leaf buds of the varieties called *aotade* or *sasatade* in vinegar or **nihaizu**. For the red variety, *see also* **benitade**.

tai たい　鯛　sea bream, mostly Family Sparidae. The Japanese have regarded sea bream as the king of fish from very early times and this attitude is reinforced by a pun on the word for congratulations, *omedetai*. *Ma-dai*, まだい　真鯛 *Pagrus major*, is representative and much in demand for weddings and other celebratory occasions. A beautiful peach-red color, it is plentiful in the Sea of Japan and in the Inland Sea, but is comparatively scarce on the Pacific side of Japan. It reaches 100 cm in length and is at its best in early spring. It is eaten as sashimi and **yakimono** and makes a fitting **wandane** for **suimono**.

tairagi たいらぎ　玉珧　fan shell, pen shell, sea pen *Actrina pectinata*. Popularly called *tairagai*, it can be quite a large shellfish, up to 36 cm long. It is found throughout Japan south of northern Honshu, being in season from December to February. The adductor muscle (**kaibashira**) is eaten as sashimi and in **sunomono** and is good as **furai** or grilled with **uni** (*uniyaki*).

taishō ebi たいしょうえび　大正海老　fleshy prawn *Penaeus chinensis*. *See also* **ebi**.

taiyaki たいやき　鯛焼き　sea-bream-shaped cake. This popular snack is a **tai**-shaped batter cake made in an iron mold and filled with **an**. It is very popular with children and is usually found at festivals.

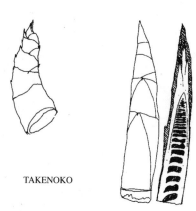

TAKENOKO

taka no tsume たかのつめ 鷹の爪 cayenne pepper, chili pepper, tabasco pepper *Capsicum annuum* var. *conoides*. This is a very hot variety of chili pepper.

takenoko たけのこ 竹の子、 筍 bamboo shoot, usually the shoots of *mōsō chiku* 孟宗竹 *Phyllostachys heterocycla* var. *pubescens*. The shoots of *ma-dake* 真竹 *Phyllostachys bambusoides* are also sometimes used. The young shoots of bamboo, mostly appearing in late spring, but in some varieties in autumn, are eaten as a vegetable. The shoot is first boiled and then used in any way desired. Bamboo shoot prepared as **aemono** with **kinome** is excellent.

tako たこ 蛸、 章魚 octopus *Octopus vulgaris*. mizudako, madako *Paroctopus dofleini*. iidako *Polypus fangsias*. Winter and early spring is the best time for most kinds of octopus, but a lot of it is frozen, to be eaten year-round, since it is so popular. It is always eaten cooked, even on sushi. Most commonly served as **sunomono**, it is also prepared as **aemono** with **karashi sumiso**, and with soy sauce flavored with **wasabi** (*takowasa*).

takoyaki たこやき 蛸焼き chopped octopus in batter cooked into ball shapes in an iron mold, served with thickened **usutā sōsu**, and eaten with a toothpick. It is a simple, popular snack requiring strong powers of digestion.

TAKO

takuan zuke たくあんづけ 沢庵漬け pickled **daikon** radish. Basically a kind of *nukazuke* (for which *see also* **tsukemono**) colored yellow with turmeric (**ukon**), it was supposedly invented in the seventeenth century by the Zen monk Takuan Soho. Homemade *takuan* can be very good indeed, whereas the widespread commercial product is often extremely unpleasant. *Takuan* is the most ubiquitous of all Japanese pickles.

tamago たまご 卵 egg. Unless otherwise specified, *tamago* means hen's egg, *keiran* けいらん 鶏卵. The other egg in common use is quail's egg. Eggs are extensively used in Japanese cooking and are often eaten raw at breakfast. *Yude tamago* is hard-boiled egg and *hanjuku tamago* is soft-boiled.

tamago dōfu たまごどうふ 卵豆腐 egg tofu. Block-shaped, firm, savory egg custard made with **dashi**, it is usually chilled and served with soy sauce thinned with **dashi** (*warijōyu*). It is a light and refreshing dish valued by many vegetarians.

tamagoyaki たまごやき 卵焼き Japanese-style omelet. Eggs are lightly beaten with **dashi**, soy sauce, and sugar or **mirm** and cooked in a rectangular pan so that the omelet can be rolled up in a rectangular shape, without any wasteful trimming. Sushi chefs do wondrous things in this way, having special bamboo mats to shape **datemaki**, an egg topping for sushi.

tamajakushi たまじゃくし 玉杓子 soup ladle. *See also* **o-tama-jakushi**.

tamanegi たまねぎ 玉葱、葱頭 onion *Allium cepa*. Round onions, as distinct from welsh onions (**negi**), have quite a minor place in Japanese food. They are sometimes used for **aemono** with a dressing of cod's roe (*tarako ae*) or sesame (*goma ae*) and are often included in the more hearty soups, such as **satsumajiru**.

tamari たまり 溜まり soy sauce made without wheat. *See also* Appendix 10.

tanishi たにし 田螺 vivipara (a kind of water snail) *Cipangopaludina chinensis nalleata*. These snails, which proliferate in the rice fields and marshlands all over Japan, are a good source of protein, but are hardly eaten outside the areas where they are found, and even there are probably not consumed to any great extent. They can be put in **miso shiru** as is, or boiled, taken out of their shells, and prepared as **aemono** with a dressing of **kinome** or **sumiso**.

tanpopo たんぽぽ 蒲公英 dandelion *Taraxacum platycarpum*. The European dandelion has now well overtaken the Japanese native. In either case, young spring leaves are plucked and blanched and used for **aemono** or **o-hitashi**.

tara たら 鱈、大口魚 cod *Gadus macrocephalus* (ma-dara). Attaining a length of 1 m, this fish inhabits the cold northern waters and is at its best during the spawning season in winter. For sashimi it must be straight out of the sea. Otherwise, it is good in **chirinabe** and as **shioyaki**.

tarabagani たらばがに 鱈場蟹 king crab *Paralithodes camtschaticus*. With a carapace 25 cm wide and long legs, this crab makes a spread of over 1 m. As its name, literally cod-place crab, implies, it inhabits the cod-fishing areas off Hokkaido, with a life span of twenty years. The season is limited from November to March and a lot of the catch is canned. After boiling, it makes excellent **sunomono** (*kanisu*) and salads.

tarako たらこ 鱈子 cod's roe. A loose way of referring to **mentaiko**.

tare たれ 垂れ sauce. Soy sauce or miso is sweetened with sugar or **mirin**, and crushed garlic or sesame seeds may be added. This sauce is mostly used as a dip for **nabemono**, **yakiniku**, and **teppanyaki**.

tataki たたき 叩き 1. a method of preparing fish by mincing it finely with a knife. It is seasoned with ginger, **negi**, and **shiso** and served with a dip of soy sauce with grated ginger. 2. *tataki* of bonito or beef. The mincing is omitted and the fillet is briefly grilled, leaving the inside raw. It is then sliced like sashimi and served with the same dip as above. This is justifiably considered the best way of eating bonito raw. The flavors of bonito and beef are remarkably similar.

tatami iwashi たたみいわし 畳鰯 *Engraulis japonica*. The fry of anchovies (**katakuchi iwashi**) sun-dried on rectangular grids. They are eaten with soy sauce after lightly toasting.

tatsuta-age たつたあげ 竜田揚げ chicken, whitefish, or whale meat marinated in saké or **mirin** with soy sauce, then dusted with **kuzu** or **katakuriko**, and deep-fried. Served with grated ginger or **daikon**.

tawashi たわし 束子 kitchen brush. A fist-shaped brush traditionally made of hemp-palm fiber or rice straw, excellent for scrubbing vegetables. The word is also currently used for similar brushes made of nylon or steel wool.

teba てば 手羽 (chicken) wing. The whole wing is referred to as *tebamoto*, and the wingtip is *tebasaki*. Deep-fried and served with black pepper and salt, they are a great favorite at **yakitori** establishments. Wings are mostly skin and bone, though the flesh is sweet.

teishoku ていしょく 定食 set meal, fixed menu. Where more than one set meal is available, it is usual to distinguish them by letters of the alphabet: A ランチ (lunch or *ranchi* in Japanese), B ランチ, and so on. The Japanese word *ranchi* does not necessarily refer to midday.

tekkamaki てっかまき 鉄火巻き **norimaki** of tunny (**maguro**) and **wasabi**.

tendon てんどん 天丼 tempura on rice as a **donburi**.

tengusa てんぐさ 天草 agar-agar, Ceylon moss *Gelidium amansii*. This is the seaweed from which **kanten** is made.

tenpura てんぷら 天婦羅、天麩羅 seafood and vegetables deep-fried in batter, fritters. The Japanese quest for perfection in food, primarily sought through attention to detail and achieved with artistic flair, is above all experienced at the counter of a good tempura restaurant. The basic method of cooking was introduced in the sixteenth century by the Portuguese, and the techniques have been refined down the centuries. The quality and formula of the oil, its temperature, the formula of the flour for the batter, and the degree of mixing are all important. The timing is so important that it is necessary to sit immediately in front of the chef for the best results. The primary ingredient is large prawns (*saimaki ebi*) but squid and **shiromizakana** are much used. Vegetables such as **satsumaimo** are very good. The leaves and young buds of **shiso** are very good, and young carrot leaves, **shishitō**, and **pīman** are also used, The fritters are dipped into a clear soup (**tentsuyu**) into which are mixed the grated **daikon** and ginger with which the diner is provided. Alternatively, salt may be used, or lemon juice.

tentsuyu てんつゆ 天汁 clear dipping broth for tempura. It consists of **dashi** flavored with soy sauce and **mirin** and is served hot.

teppan てっぱん 鉄板 iron hot plate. It is used for grilling **teppanyaki** and **okonomiyaki**.

teppanyaki てっぱんやき 鉄板焼き slices of meat and vegetables grilled on an iron hot plate and served with **tare** as a dip. It is not usual in Japan for the chef to put on a display of knife juggling, unless for the benefit of parties of foreign tourists.

teriyaki てりやき　照り焼き　luster grilling. Fish, chicken, and vegetables are basted with soy sauce enriched with **mirin**, saké, and sugar while being grilled, to make them glisten when cooked, as well, of course, as to add flavor.

tobiuo とびうお　飛魚　flying fish *Cypselurus agoo agoo*. Found in the coastal waters of southern Japan, flying fish reach a length of 35 cm. They skim through the air 2 m above the surface of the water and can reach a distance of 400 m. Caught during the spawning season in early summer, they are grilled as **yakimono**, deep-fried as **agemono**, and are made into **chikuwa**.

tōfu とうふ　豆腐　soybean curd. A coagulant, traditionally **nigari**, is added to strained soybean milk, made by boiling ground soybeans with water. A curd is formed, which is cut into blocks and used in many ways as a most nutritious and tasty food. The residue from straining the milk, **okara**, being the pulped skins of the beans, is also very nutritious but not so tasty. The two main kinds of tofu are **momendōfu**, the regular kind, and **kinugoshidōfu**, with a much finer texture and mostly made in summer. Among the many delightful ways of serving tofu, two stand out: **yudōfu** in winter and **hiyayakko** in summer. Tofu came to Japan from China under Buddhist influence, being first recorded in Japan in A.D. 1183, and became a great standby of Zen vegetarianism (**shōjin ryōri**). However, Japanese tofu should be used wherever possible for Japanese cooking, since it is not quite the same as Chinese tofu. Some shops abroad sell both.

tōgarashi とうがらし　唐辛子　蕃椒　red pepper, chili, cayenne *Capsicum annuum* var. *conoides*. The primary ingredient, ground, of **shichimi tōgarashi**. The whole pods are also available dried, and are mostly used in pickles.

toishi といし　砥石　whetstone. At least two stones of different degrees of fineness are necessary for sharpening Japanese cooks' knives (**hōchō**). Water, not oil, is used as lubricant for this most important procedure.

tokoroten ところてん 心太 thin threads made from the gelatin (**kanten**) of seaweeds such as **tengusa** and eaten with soy sauce, vinegar, and mustard. The dish is served chilled as a popular summer snack.

tonkatsu とんカツ 豚カツ very popular dish of the **furai** category, consisting of a deep-fried slice of pork coated with egg and bread crumbs, served with a thickish *usutā-* (Worcester) style sauce and a mound of finely shredded raw cabbage. The pork is sliced for eating with chopsticks, but very often the rice is served on a plate rather than in a bowl, suggesting it is felt to be a Western dish. Specialist restaurants offer various different cuts of pork and produce a first-rate dish.

tonkotsu とんこつ 豚骨 simmered pork belly. Belly of pork with bones still attached is lightly sealed in oil, then seasoned with **shōchū** and gently simmered until the meat separates from the bones. This is followed by a long, slow simmering with miso, sugar, and saké, to which **daikon**, **gobō**, and **konnyaku** are added. It is a traditional dish of the Kagoshima area in southern Kyushu.

tori とり 鶏 *See* **wakadori**.

torigai とりがい 鳥貝 cockle *Fulvia mutica*. The shell is about 9.5 cm in length and height and 6.5 cm across. It is a favorite topping for **nigirizushi** and also makes good **sunomono**. *See also* Appendix 11.

tori motsu とりもつ 鶏もつ chicken giblets, principally the heart, liver, and gizzard. As well as being served in *motsunabe*, they can be grilled and fried.

tori niku とりにく 鶏肉 chicken (as a meat). Also pronounced *kei niku*.

toro とろ belly flesh of tuna (**maguro**). Pale in color and rich in fat, it is highly prized for sushi and sashimi. The very highly regarded middle section is called **chūtoro**.

tororo konbu とろろこんぶ とろろ昆布 1. preparation of **kon-**

bu that makes it fine and decorative. *Ma-konbu* or *rishiri konbu* is soaked in vinegar, dried, and shaved. It forms a wide, rather fragile, pale-colored ribbon that can be used instead of **nori** for wrapping **makizushi** and is also put into clear soup. 2. natural variety of *konbu* called *tororo konbu* (*Kjellmaniella aniella*).

toso とそ　屠蘇　spiced saké or **mirin**. More of a medicine than a tipple, this is saké (or *mirin*) in which *tososan* 屠蘇散 has been steeped. *Tososan* comes in triangular red silk bags and is a Chinese medicinal mixture of cinnamon, **sanshō**, and the roots of **bōfū** 防風 *Ledebouriella seseloides*, *kikyō* 桔梗 *Platycodon grandiflorum*, and *byakujutsu* (a kind of *okera*) 白朮 *Atractylodes macrocephala*. *Toso* is drunk at New Year to ensure health for the coming year and is served in specially decorated vessels.

tsuboyaki つぼやき　壺焼き　turbo or top-shell (**sazae**) grilled in the shell. The creature is removed from the shell, sliced, and returned with a little **mitsuba**, **yurine**, and **ginnan** with some well-seasoned stock. The shell's lid is replaced and the turbo is grilled.

tsubu つぶ　螺、　海螺　a kind of whelk *Neptunea arthritica*. A shellfish akin to **sazae**, which comes from Hokkaido, where it is called *ezosazae*, *ezo* referring to Hokkaido.

tsukemono つけもの　漬物　pickles. An integral part of every Japanese meal. The simplest Japanese meal consists of rice with a soup and a dish of vegetable pickles. This is *ichijū issai*, meaning one soup and one vegetable, the rice being taken for granted. Few of these pickles are intended as preserves. Some, such as *nara-zuke* and **umeboshi**, improve with keeping, but most are intended for current consumption. The main methods of pickling are the following: 1. **shiozuke**, salt pickling, the easiest and hence most popular. Vegetables are sliced, salted, and placed under a weight for varying lengths of time. This step is often a preliminary to other forms of pickling, but if not, the salt is usually washed off before serving. Very briefly made *shiozuke* is called *ichiyazuke* (one-night pickles), and the best-known long-term *shiozuke* is

umeboshi. 2. **suzuke**, vinegar pickling. Japanese vinegar is low in acidity and these pickles are not usually intended for long keeping. A notable exception is **rakkyō**, pickled scallions. 3. **nukazuke**. *Nuka* is rice bran. As a medium for pickling, it has salt and usually dried chilies added to it. The vegetables are buried in *nuka* and kept there for some time, ideally three months. The vegetables should be washed before eating. The best-known *nukazuke* is **takuan**. 4. *kasuzuke*. **Kasu** is what remains of the rice from making saké. A pickling bed is made of **sakekasu**, vodka-like white liquor, sugar, and salt. The longer the pickling lasts, the better. This is particularly true of *narazuke*, Nara City's famous pickle and the most famous *kasuzuke*. *Narazuke* is usually made with **shirouri**, eggplant, or burdock. 5. **misozuke**. As a pickling medium, miso is mixed with saké. Some pickles can be made quite quickly, but others take several days. Garlic and pumpkin make good *misozuke*, as does tofu. 6. *kōjizuke*. Rice mold (**kōji**) is used, the yeast being *Aspergillus oryzae*. Winter is the time for this kind of pickle, the best one being **bettarazuke**. 7. *shōyuzuke*. The pickling medium is soy sauce with **mirin**, and the best-known example is **fukujinzuke**. This short explanation describes seven common pickle types, but some of the best pickles are not easily categorized. The **senmaizuke** of Kyoto is a good example and is one of the pickles that should not be washed before eating.

tsukimi つきみ 月見 As a culinary term, this means that a raw egg yolk has been placed on top of a dish such as **soba** or **udon**. *Tsukimi* means moon viewing.

tsukudani つくだに 佃煮 salt-sweet preserves. Fish, shellfish, seaweed, and vegetables are simmered with a mixture of soy sauce, **mirin**, and sugar until almost dry. These preserves keep well and are appreciated for their salty-sweet flavor.

tsukune つくね 捏ね meatballs. Finely minced fish, fowl, or meat is squeezed to a paste with egg and formed into balls. These are prepared in various ways, such as **nimono**, **yakimono**, or **agemono**.

TSUKUSHI

tsukushi つくし 土筆 spore-bearing shoot of a plant called *sugina*. These shoots appear in spring and are a feature of **sansai ryōri**. After blanching well to remove the bitterness, they are prepared as **aemono**, **sunomono**, and **o-hitashi**.

tsumamimono つまみもの 摘まみ物 food to accompany drinking. Any nibble or tidbit or even more substantial food that is eaten with drinks rather than as part of a meal with rice is considered *tsumamimono*.

tsumire つみれ 摘入 **surimi** of fish bound with egg white and starch, seasoned, put by the spoonful into broth, and simmered. Yam and tofu can also be used. It can be served in a soup (*tsumire jiru*) as **wandane**.

—U—

udo うど 独活 udo *Aralia cordata*. A fragrant plant, the white stalks and leaves of which are eaten. Reminiscent of asparagus both in aroma and taste, *udo* is cultivated as well as gathered wild. Wild *udo* (*yama udo*) belongs to **sansai ryōri** and must be blanched before use. It has a stronger flavor than cultivated *udo*, which is blanched by being grown in the dark. The tender young

UDO

stems, available throughout the year but best in spring, can be eaten raw and are used for **suimono**, **sunomono**, **aemono**, and **o-hitashi**.

udon うどん 饂飩 soft, thick wheat noodles. These popular noodles are eaten fresh, served in bowls of broth with accompaniments such as **abura-age** (in the dish called *kitsune udon*) or tempura (in *tenpura udon*). *Tenpura udon* should not be confused with **tendon**, which is *tenpura donburi*, a rice dish.

udonsuki うどんすき 饂飩鋤 **nabemono** in which **udon** is cooked in a pot full of light, clear soup with chicken or fish and vegetables.

uirō ういろう 外郎 firm, gelatinous, block-shaped confection made of rice flour or **kuzu** and colored and flavored with powdered green tea or **an** of **azuki**.

ukon うこん 鬱金 turmeric *Curcuma domestica*. Powdered turmeric is used to give **takuan zuke** a good yellow color, and is used in curry powder for its aroma.

umami うまみ 旨味 *See* Appendix 14.

ume うめ 梅 Japanese apricot *Prunus mume* (*Armeniaca mume*). This little early-summer fruit, often erroneously referred to as the Japanese plum, has two main uses. It is macerated in alcohol with rock sugar to make the delicious liqueur **umeshu**, or salt-pickled to make **umeboshi**.

UNI

umeboshi うめぼし 梅干し dried, salt-pickled Japanese apricot. These apricots come large and small, soft and hard, and are an item of daily consumption. Usually colored red with red **shiso** leaves, they are mostly eaten as a pickle with rice, but the large soft ones, desalted by soaking in water, make very good tempura. A cup of **bancha** tea containing an *umeboshi* makes a good start to the morning. A **bentō** with an *umeboshi* on top of the rice is called *hinomaru bentō*, after the Japanese flag. Rice gruel (**kayu**), a breakfast food, is usually served with *umeboshi*.

umeshu うめしゅ 梅酒 liqueur made by macerating **ume** in alcohol with rock sugar. It has a very strong taste of bitter almonds from the Prussic acid in the stones, but is not poisonous. In summer it is drunk to alkalize the blood and in winter, to soothe sore throats. The production is usually domestic, families being very proud of their own product.

unagi うなぎ 鰻 eel *Anguilla japonica*. Born in the sea, this eel migrates to rivers and lakes throughout most of Japan, growing to about 50 cm in length, and is extensively cultivated as a freshwater fish. It has no special season, but is particularly eaten in the height of summer (as *doyō unagi*) because of its high-energy nutritional value. One of the best ways of eating eel is as **kabayaki**, but it is also served in other ways, such as **nabemono** (as *unabe*) and **donburi** (as *unadon*).

unagi no kabayaki うなぎのかばやき 鰻の蒲焼 *See* **kabayaki**.

uni うに 海胆、海栗、雲丹 sea urchin Class Echinoidea var. genera. The orange-yellow ovaries are a great treat, being one of

USU   HIKIUSU

the top three delicacies (*tenka no san dai chinmi*). *Uni* can be eaten raw, is used as a topping for **nigirizushi** (for which *see also* Appendix 11), and is very good mixed with egg yolk as a topping for grilled seafood (*uniyaki*). It also makes an outstanding **koromo** for **aemono** (*uniae*) of abalone (**awabi**), jellyfish (**kurage**), and salted herring roe (**kazunoko**). In western Japan **shiokara** of *uni* is prepared on a large scale.

unohana うのはな　卯の花　polite culinary term for **o-kara**.

uoshōyu うおしょうゆ　魚醤油　fish **shōyu**. The label "fish sauce," the name given to *uoshōyu* by way of translation in the Southeast Asian countries where it is found, conjures up entirely the wrong idea. *Uoshōyu* is a salty, golden-colored, clear liquid, the product of the fermentation of small fish with salt. The Romans used it as their basic condiment, calling it *garum* or *liquamen* in Latin. Currently it is an essential of the cooking of Thailand, Cambodia, Laos, and the Philippines, and until the introduction of soy sauce from China, probably in the mid thirteenth century, was of Japan also. It is still made in parts of Japan, that of Akita being called *shottsuru*. *Shottsuru nabe*, containing **hatahata**, tofu, and vegetables in stock seasoned with **shottsuru**, is a famous **nabemono**. Many people are put off by the fishy smell of *uoshōyu*, but when used discreetly it transforms almost anything for the good, because of its high level of **umami** (for which *see also* Appendix 14). The *ikanago shōyu* of Kagawa Prefecture is another famous *uoshōyu*. High-quality *uoshōyu*, called *nam pla* in Thai, is made in Thailand.

uragoshi うらごし 裏漉し *See* **koshiki**.

uri うり 瓜 cucurbit, gourd, melon. As a vegetable, this includes **kyūri** (cucumber) and **shirouri** (Oriental pickling melon); as fruit, melons, including watermelon (**suika**).

uruka うるか 鱁鮧 entrails of **ayu** prepared as **shiokara**. *See also* **wata**.

usu うす 臼 mortar, mill, of which there are two main kinds. 1. *Tsukiusu* is a large mortar standing on the ground, made either of wood or stone. It is currently mostly used for making **mochi** by pounding steamed glutinous rice into a paste. In the past it was used for husking and polishing rice. 2. *Hikiusu* is a stone mill with upper and lower millstones, used for grinding rice flour and soybean flour.

usugiri うすぎり 薄切り sliced thinly. An example is thinly sliced cucumber in **sunomono**.

usutā sōsu ウスターソース Worcester sauce, Worcestershire sauce. Based on the original Lea and Perrins' sauce, which was based on an Anglo-Indian recipe from India and brought to Japan in the second half of the nineteenth century. The Japanese version is not quite so pungent. It has become so popular that cafeterias and other simple restaurants place it on the table next to the soy sauce.

usuzukuri うすづくり 薄作り、 薄造り thin slicing. This is a sashimi term with reference to firm-fleshed fish such as **fugu** and implies careful, decorative arrangement of the slices on a dish.

uzura うずら 鶉 quail *Coturnix coturnix*. Occupying a fairly minor position in Japanese cuisine, it is mostly used in high-class cookery but can also be served grilled and in **nabemono**. Fresh quail's eggs (*uzura no tamago*) are found in every supermarket. Being small (3 cm), they can be used whole, hard-boiled, to decorative effect. Raw and minus the shell, they are placed on a bed of grated yam (**yamanoimo**) and consumed with soy sauce in the dish called *tsukimi tororo*.

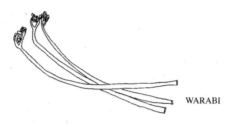

WARABI

—W—

wagashi わがし 和菓子 the Japanese equivalent of confectionary, cakes, cookies, and candy. However, the category of *wagashi* defies translation since it does not correspond to anything in Western culture. The three groups are *namagashi* 生菓子, *han namagashi* 半生菓子, and **higashi** 干菓子. *Namagashi*, literally raw **kashi**, are mostly made from various sweet raw pastes filled with **an**. The beauty of the design is all important, except for such confections as **uirō** and **yōkan**. Like most *wagashi*, their function is to overcome the bitterness of tea-ceremony tea (**matcha**) with their sweetness. *Han namagashi*, as the name, literally half-raw *kashi*, implies, are less moist than *namagashi*. They include *amanatto* (crystallized **sasage** or other beans), **kibidango**, and **kasutera**. *Higashi* includes candy and crackers, for which *see also* **higashi**.

wagiri わぎり 輪切り sliced rounds of **daikon** or carrot.

wakadori わかどり 若鶏 chicken *Gallus gallus domesticus*. Cheap, versatile, and very popular. *Tori no teriyaki* and **yakitori** are basic to Japanese food life.

wakame わかめ 若布、和布 wakame *Undaria pinnitifida*. Mainly used in miso soup, this seaweed has many other uses, including **sunomono** and **nuta**.

wakasagi わかさぎ 若鷺、公魚 pond smelt *Hypomesus nipponensis*. Like **ayu**, its relative, this fish divides its life between the

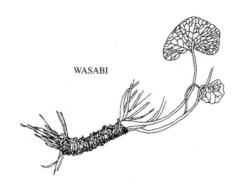

WASABI

sea, brackish waters, and rivers, though some also live in lakes. It grows to about 15 cm. It is often dried on skewers and then deep-fried as **kara-age**. Fresh, it is cooked as tempura and **furai** and prepared in various ways with vinegar.

wakegi わけぎ 分葱 *Allium wakegi*. A very useful autumn "spring" onion. The green is sliced and used as a flavoring in soups, dips, and other dishes.

wan わん 椀 bowl for serving food. Many foods are served in bowls rather than on plates. The bowl for rice and soup is the **cha-wan**, and that for powdered green tea is *matcha jawan*.

wandane わんだね 椀種 the main ingredient of soup or other food served in a **wan**.

wankosoba わんこそば 椀子蕎麦 *See* **soba**.

wanzuma わんづま 椀妻 the helper or "wife" of the **wandane**. Often a colorful vegetable, it is intended to complement the *wan-dane* and add color.

warabi わらび 蕨 bracken *Pteridium aquilinum* var. *latiusculum*. A great standby of **sansai ryōri**, it has to be well blanched before being used. It is used in soup, **o-hitashi**, **aemono**, and **nimono**. The young, uncoiled fronds are croziers.

waribashi わりばし 割箸 disposable wooden chopsticks coming in the piece. They must be pulled apart before use and are used again only in very informal circumstances. The inexperienced often find *waribashi* more difficult to use than regular domestic chopsticks.

warishita わりした 割下 **dashi** flavored with soy sauce and **mirin**. It is mainly used in **nabemono**.

wasabi わさび 山葵 wasabi *Wasabia japonica*. A fellow member of the Family Cruciferae with horseradish, it is very similar in flavor, though less harsh and more aromatic. Wild, it grows in cool, shaded, shallow streams of very pure water, high in the mountains. It is also extensively cultivated. Either way, it is expensive. The popular powder is a cheap substitute of horseradish colored green with some mustard added. *Wasabi* is mainly used with sushi and sashimi. *See also* Appendix 16.

wasabi daikon わさびだいこん 山葵大根 horseradish *Armoracia rusticana*. Although not really an ingredient of traditional Japanese food, dried, powdered horseradish colored green is extensively used as a substitute for the much more expensive **wasabi**. Abroad, most people who think they are enjoying *wasabi* are actually eating disguised horseradish. Also called **seiyōwasabi**.

wasabizuke わさびづけ 山葵漬け **sakekasu** pickle of **wasabi** sometimes containing **kazunoko**. Strongly recommended.

wasanbon わさんぼん 和三盆 wasanbon sugar. This very high-quality sugar is handmade from the comparatively slender Chinese sugar cane *Saccharum sinense*, called in Japanese *chikusha* ちくしゃ 竹蔗. The name *wasanbon* derives from the three (nowadays four) kneadings used to extract the invert syrup from the raw sugar. Most of the very limited amount produced is used by top-quality confectioners in Kyoto. *See also* Appendix 17.

washoku わしょく 和食 traditional Japanese food or meal. The term excludes most Western and Chinese dishes commonly eaten in Japan as well as such dishes as curry and rice, *karē raisu* カレーライス.

wata わた　腸　entrails of seafood and fowl. Many are made into **shiokara**, famous ones being **uruka** of **ayu** and **konowata** of **namako**.

wata-ame わたあめ　綿飴　*See* **watagashi**.

watagashi わたがし　綿菓子　spun sugar, candy floss, cotton candy. A popular favorite of children at festivals, though hardly a traditional Japanese confection. Also called **wata-ame**.

watarigani わたりがに　渡り蟹　blue swimmer *Portunus trituberculatus*. This bluish-green crab is prolific in Tokyo and Ise bays and the Ariake Sea. Measuring 15 cm across, it is in season from January to April with abundant crab meat that is delicious.

—Y—

yaki- 焼-　grilled, used as a prefix as in the following entries.

yakidōfu やきどうふ　焼き豆腐　grilled tofu. It is used in sukiyaki and other **nabemono** as well as in **nimono**.

yakiimo やきいも　焼き芋　*See* **ishiyaki imo**.

yakimeshi やきめし　焼き飯　fried rice. A Chinese dish, also called *chāhan* チャーハン. It is a good, though not Japanese, way of using up cooked rice.

yakimono やきもの　焼き物　grilled foods. A simple but very effective way of cooking many foods, ideally done over charcoal. Grilling can be done on a griddle (*yakiami*), **teppan**, or *tōban* 陶板 (glazed pottery tile or plate) over the **konro** or **shichirin**, or on a stake at the **irori**, though it seems that direct grilling over charcoal is carcinogenic. One of the best ways of cooking fish is **shioyaki**. Other methods of grilling include teriyaki, **kabayaki**, and *kushiyaki* (grilling on skewers).

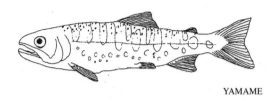

YAMAME

yakiniku やきにく 焼き肉 grilled meat. It is cooked on a griddle, often over charcoal, and eaten with vegetables cooked the same way. There are many specialist *yakiniku* restaurants.

yakinori やきのり 焼き海苔 *See* **nori**.

yakitori やきとり 焼き鳥 bite-size pieces of chicken grilled on a skewer. Many parts of the chicken, including the skin and the gizzard, are used. Other birds are also used, especially sparrow, the head being crunched whole. *Yakitori* is a very popular **tsumami-mono** and many simple drinking places specialize in it.

yakumi やくみ 薬味 herbs and spices used as a condiment. A common example is **shichimi tōgarashi**.

yama fugu やまふぐ 山河豚 sashimi of **konnyaku**. White *konnyaku* is sliced thinly and eaten with a dip of **karashi sumiso**.

yamaimo やまいも 山芋、薯蕷 *See* **yamanoimo**.

yamakake やまかけ 山掛け grated **yamanoimo** placed on top of seafood, usually cubes of tuna, and eaten with various seasonings, including **wasabi** and soy sauce. Also called *yamaimokake* やまいもかけ 山芋掛け.

yamame やまめ 山女 *See* **masu 1**.

yamanoimo やまのいも 山の芋 薯蕷 yam *Dioscorea japonica*. The wild yam is *jinenjo* 自然薯, and several varieties such as the long **nagaimo** and *ichōimo* 銀杏薯 (shaped like a ginkgo leaf) are extensively cultivated. At their best from November but suitable for grating in September and October, they are used in many ways, especially **sunomono** and **agemono**. Grated yam, which

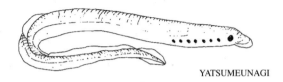

YATSUMEUNAGI

has a very slippery texture, is called *tororo* and is used in *tororo jiru* (a soup) and *tsukimi tororo*, for which *see also* **uzura**. *Yamanoimo* is also called **yamaimo**.

yanagawanabe やながわなべ　柳川鍋　one-pot dish of **dojō** and **gobō**. *Gobō* is arranged in the bottom of a **donabe**, and *dojō* that have been cleaned, boned, and beheaded are placed on top with a sweet rich stock. When cooked, this is served with soft-boiled eggs on top and a sprinkling of **sanshō**.

yasai やさい　野菜　vegetable.

yatai やたい　屋台　stall. Whenever there is a festival, whether of a shrine or a town or a college, stalls are set up and popular foods such as **takoyaki** prepared on the spot and sold. Stalls are also found nightly near railway stations and on the fringes of entertainment districts, with much more emphasis placed on drinking. There is usually provision for a small number of people to sit at the counter and socialize. At such stalls **rāmen** is very popular. The full term is *yataimise* やたいみせ　屋台店.

yatsuhashi やつはし　八つ橋　Kyoto confection made of rice flour and sugar and flavored with cinnamon. As well as the crisp **senbei** type, there is a raw type (*nama yatsuhashi*), which is steamed, stuffed with **an**, and still soft when eaten.

yatsumeunagi やつめうなぎ　八目鰻　lamprey *Lampetra japonica* (kawa-yatsume). Living in the rivers of central and northern Japan, lampreys grow to over 60 cm long. As a very rich source of vitamin A, they have long been considered good medicine for night blindness. Best grilled as **kabayaki**.

yōkan ようかん 羊羹 sweet red-bean (**azuki**) confection. A kind of **namagashi** made of **an**, sugar, and agar-agar (**kanten**) or **kuzu**. It can be flavored with persimmon (**kaki 2**) or powdered green tea (**matcha**) and is served at the tea ceremony. *See also* **wagashi** and Appendix 13.

yomogi よもぎ 蓬、艾 mugwort *Artemisia princeps*. A ubiquitous weed considered very healthy. In spring the young leaves are blanched and made into **o-hitashi** or added to soups or rice. *Kusamochi* is a kind of **mochi** that is colored green and flavored with *yomogi*. *Kusa* means grass, herb, or weed. *Yomogi* is also dried and used as moxa in moxibustion.

yosenabe よせなべ 寄せ鍋 one-pot dish in which you put whatever you like into flavored soup stock. The stock in the diner's individual bowl is flavored with sharp citrus juice of some kind and **shichimi tōgarashi**.

yuba ゆば 湯葉 soy-milk skin. A speciality of Kyoto, this skin that is formed when soy milk (*tōnyū* 豆乳) is heated is not only delicious, but highly nutritious, being the richest source of protein known (over 52%). It is also high in natural sugars (12%) and polyunsaturated fats (24%) and therefore very high in energy. It is eaten both fresh and dried, being added to soups and used as a skin to roll up such things as cucumber and burdock. Nearly all *yuba* is made in Kyoto and it is fairly expensive. Much use is made of *yuba* in **shōjin ryōri**.

yude- ゆで- 茹で- prefix meaning boiled, derived from *yuderu*. Thus, *yudetamago* means hard-boiled egg.

yuderu ゆでる 茹でる the culinary process of boiling.

yudōfu ゆどうふ 湯豆腐 hot tofu. A winter dish in which large cubes of tofu are heated in simmering water with **konbu** and then dipped into a hot, soy-based dip and eaten with **yakumi** such as grated ginger or **daikon**, shaved **katsuobushi**, and finely sliced spring onion green. Nanzen-ji, a great Zen temple in Kyoto, is

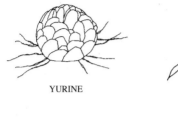

YURINE

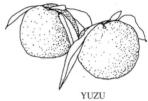

YUZU

famous for the large number of surrounding restaurants that specialize in this excellent dish.

yūgao ゆうがお　夕顔　white-flowered gourd *Lagenaria siceraria* var. *hispida*. The gourd from which **kanpyō** is made.

yurine ゆりね　百合根　lily root *Lilium* spp. The delightful crunchy, waxy texture of the edible lily root makes it a good addition to **chawan mushi**. It is also used in **nimono**.

yuzu ゆず　柚　Japanese citron *Citrus junos*. *Yuzu* is used mostly for the zest, which has an unforgettably delicate citrus aroma. Slivers of zest are put in **suimono** and **chawan mushi**. Dried, *yuzu* is sometimes added to **shichimi tōgarashi**. The juice is mixed with vinegar and soy sauce to make a dip (*yuzu ponzu*) for one-pot dishes such as **yudōfu** and **shabu shabu**.

—Z—

zabon ザボン　朱欒、香欒　pomelo, shaddock (from Portuguese *zamboa*, meaning pomelo or shaddock). *See also* **buntan**.

zarigani ざりがに　蝲蛄　freshwater crayfish 1. native Japanese *Cambaroides japonicus*. 2. American red swamp crawfish *Procambarus clarkii*. The native Japanese crayfish is restricted to the

ZARIGANI (Japapanese)   ZARIGANI (American)

northern parts of Japan, whereas the American introduction has spread throughout the country. With a body about 10 cm long, they are tasty, and can be prepared in all the same ways as prawns; however, they are inclined to harbor parasites and must be very well cooked. Although the American introduction is referred to as crawfish, in careful usage, small freshwater lobsters are referred to as crayfish. Crawfish is the spiny lobster, a marine crustacean.

zaru ざる 笊 bamboo colander. It can also be made of plastic or metal.

zarusoba ざるそば 笊蕎麦 *See* **soba**.

zen ぜん 膳 low, individual table for dining. Used for formal Japanese-style dining, these trays-on-legs used to indicate social status by their several designs. At formal dinners it is not exceptional for diners to have three *zen* each. With the introduction of the communal low-legged table last century, the use of the zen has declined considerably. *See also* **oshiki**.

zenmai ぜんまい 薇 royal fern *Osmunda japonica*. An important plant of **sansai ryōri**, it is very similar to **warabi** but grows larger and stronger. It must be well blanched before use in **aemono**, **nimono**, tempura, and soups. The young unopened fronds are fiddleheads.

ZENMAI

zensai ぜんさい　前菜　small, attractive appetizers served at the beginning of a meal.

zenzai ぜんざい　善哉　sweet red-bean (**azuki**) soup. Toasted **mochi** are served in a sweet soup of **an**. The type of *an* used varies with the part of Japan.

zōni ぞうに　雑煮　**mochi** in soup. An important New Year dish of *mochi* in vegetable soup. The recipe for the soup varies considerably throughout the country.

zōsui ぞうすい　雑炊　rice gruel with fish and vegetables. A favorite way of making *zōsui* is to allow rice to cook in the richly flavored stock and vegetables remaining from **nabemono**. Any seafood or fowl may be added. Also called **o-jiya**.

zuwaigani ずわいがに　ずわい蟹　Pacific snow crab, queen crab *Chionoecetes opilio*. A large crab of excellent flavor, it is taken in winter off the coast of the Sea of Japan. It is served as sashimi and tempura and in various preparations with vinegar. *See also* **matsubagani**.

English–Japanese

Notes: Abbreviations appearing in this section are adj. for adjective, n. for noun, and v. for verb. Words in boldface appear in the Japanese-English section with their forms in written Japanese.

A

abalone **awabi**

adlay **hatomugi**

agar-agar **kanten**

a la carte **ippin ryōri**

anchovy **katakuchi iwashi**

angler fish **ankō**

appetizer **zensai**

apple *ringo* りんご

apricot 1. (European or Middle Eastern) **anzu** 2. (Japanese)
  ume

ark shell **akagai**

arrowhead **kuwai**

arrowroot *arōrūto* アロールート. Suitable substitutes are **kuzu**
  and **katakuriko**.

aubergine **nasu**

B

baking sheet *tenpan* 天板

baking soda *jūtansan natoriumu* 重炭酸ナトリウム, *jūsō*
  じゅうそう 重曹

bamboo shoot **takenoko**

barley **ōmugi**, **mugi**

barracuda **kamasu**

basil *bajiriko* バジリコ

bass **suzuki**

batter (for tempura) **koromo**

bay leaf *rōrie* ローリエ, *gekkeiju no ha* げっけいじゅのは
  月桂樹の葉

bay scallop **itayagai**

bean **mame**

bean curd **tōfu**

bean sprout **moyashi**, **mame moyashi**

beef **gyū niku**

bell pepper **pīman**

bicarbonate of soda *See* baking soda.

bitter orange **daidai**

black bream **kurodai**, **chinu**

black-eyed pea **sasage**

blackfish (large-type) **mejina**

black pepper *kurokoshō*

blanch *yugaku* 湯搔く, *yudōshi suru* 湯通しする, *akunuki suru* 灰汁抜きする

blood clam **akagai**

blowfish **fugu**

blue swimmer **gazami**, **watarigani**

boar 1. (animal) **inoshishi** 2. (meat) *botan niku* ぼたん肉, 牡丹肉

bone *hone* 骨

bonito **katsuo**

bowl 1. (small, for **matcha** or rice) **chawan** 2. (for composite rice dishes) **donburi** 3. (straight-sided) *hachi* 鉢

bracken **warabi**

bran *fusuma* 麩

bread *pan* パン. Long loaves are divided into *kin* 斤, a traditional weight of about 600 gm. However, in current usage one *kin* is about 12 cm of bread, weighing 400 gm or so; today length rather than weight is the criterion. *See also* loaf of bread.

bread crumbs **panko**

breakfast **chōshoku**, *asagohan* 朝御飯

broad bean **soramame**

broth **dashi**, **dashijiru**

brown rice **genmai**

brown sugar 1. (dark) *kurozatō* 黒砂糖 2. (light) *san on tō* 三温糖

Brussels sprouts *mekyabetsu* 芽キャベツ, *supurauto* スプラウト

buckwheat flour **sobako**
buffet **baikingu ryōri**, *risshoku* 立食, *byuffe* ビュッフェ
burdock **gobō**

C

cabbage *kyabetsu* キャベツ
candy **ame**
capsicum **piiman**
carp **koi**
carrot **ninjin**
catfish **namazu**
cayenne pepper **taka no tsume, tōgarashi**
chef 1. (head cook) **itamae** 2. (qualified cook) **chōrishi**
cherry **sakuranbo**
chestnut **kuri**
chicken **wakadori, niwatori**, *chikin* チキン
chili pepper **tōgarashi**
Chinese cabbage **hakusai**
chopsticks **hashi**
citron **yuzu**
citrus *kankitsurui* 柑橘類
clam (short-necked) **asari**
clove *chōji* ちょうじ 丁子, 丁字
cockle **torigai**
cinnamon *nikkei* 肉桂
cod **tara**
confectioner's sugar *konazatō* 粉砂糖
conger eel **anago**
corn (sweet) *tōmorokoshi* とうもろこし
cornflour *kōnfurawā* コーンフラワー. Since it is not readily
    available in Japan, superior substitutes are **katakuriko** (potato
    starch) and **kuzu**.
corn starch *See* cornflour.

cowpea **sasage**

crab **kani**

crawfish (marine) **ise ebi**

crayfish (freshwater) **zarigani**

croquette *korokke* コロッケ

cucumber **kyūri**

cuisine **ryōri**

curry powder **karē ko**

cutlass fish **tachiuo**

cuttlefish **kōika**

D

deep-fry *ageru* 揚げる

demerara sugar *san on tō* 三温糖

dinner *yūshoku* 夕食

dish (plate) **sara**

duck 1. (farmed) *aigamo* あいがも 合鴨, 間鴨 2. (wild) **kamo**

E

eel **unagi**

egg **tamago**

eggplant **nasu**

egg white *shiromi* 白身

egg yolk *kimi* 黄身

escabèche **nanbanzuke**

F

fermentation **hakkō**

fiddlehead *kusasotetsu* くさそてつ 草蘇鉄, *kogomi* こごみ 屈み.
  See also Appendix 9.

fig **ichijiku**

fillet (of beef or pork) *hire* ヒレ, *fire* フィレ

filleting (of fish) **sanmaioroshi**

fish **sakana 2**

fish paste **surimi**

flathead **kochi**

flavor *aji* 味

flavoring **chōmiryō**

flounder **karei**

flour (wheat) 1. *komugiko* 小麦粉 2. *merikenko* メリケン粉.
  From the beginning of the Meiji era (1868), this term was used
  for the flour imported, mostly from America, for making baked
  goods, to distinguish it from the locally produced flour for making noodles. The term is still heard, but the distinction is lost.

flying fish **tobiuo**

fruit *kudamono* くだもの 果物. Usually sold by the mound
  (*yama* 山) on a plate, except at supermarkets.

G

garfish **sayori**

garlic **ninniku**

garlic stem *kuki ninniku* 茎大蒜

gelatin *zerachin* ゼラチン

ginger **shōga**

ginkgo nut **ginnan**

glutinous rice **mochigome**

goby **haze**

gourd **uri**

grain **mugi**

grape **budō**

grate *orosu* 下ろす

grater **oroshigane**

greasy *aburakkoi* 脂っこい

green (unripe) *jukusanai* 熟さない
green bean **sayaingen**
grill 1. (cooking apparatus) *yakiami* 焼き網 2. (cooking method) *amiyaki* 網焼き
ground meat *hiki niku* 挽肉
grouper **hata**
gruel **kayu**, **zōsui**

H

hairtail **tachiuo**
halfbeak **sayori**
halibut **ohyō**
herb **kōsō**
herring **nishin**
hog (pork) **buta niku**
honey **hachimitsu**
horse mackerel **aji**
horse meat **sakura niku**, *ba niku* 馬肉
horseradish **wasabi daikon**, **seiyōwasabi**

I

ice *kōri* こおり 氷. *See also* shaved ice.
icing sugar *konazatō* 粉砂糖
ingredient *shokuzai* 食材

J

jack **aji**
jellyfish **kurage**
John Dory **matōdai**

K

kelp **konbu**
kidney bean **ingenmame**
king crab **tarabagani**
kitchen **daidokoro**
knife (cook's) **hōchō**
kumquat **kinkan**

L

lactic acid *nyū san* 乳酸
ladle **o-tamajakushi**, **tamajakushi**
lamb *ramu* ラム, *kohitsuji* 子羊
lamprey **yatsumeunagi**
laver **nori**
leatherjacket **kawahagi**
leek **negi**
lees **sakekasu**
lily root **yurine**
liver *rebā* レバー, *kanzō* 肝臓
loach **dojō**
loaf of bread *Ikkin* 一斤 (one *kin*) is a 10-to-12-cm section of a
    long loaf. The number on a pack of sliced bread indicates the
    number of slices per *kin*. Eight slices per *kin* being a suitable
    number for toast, a pack of toast bread would be *ikkin hachi
    mai giri* 一斤八枚切り. Bread, either as a loaf or sliced, is often
    called *shokupan* 食パン.
lobster 1. (spiny lobster, crawfish) **ise ebi** 2. (Atlantic lobster,
    farmed in Hokkaido) *omāru ebi* オマールえび, *robusutā*
    ロブスター
loquat **biwa**
lotus root **renkon**
low-fat milk *tei shibō nyū* 低脂肪乳

luderick **mejina**
lunch **chūshoku**, *hiru gohan* 昼御飯, *ranchi* ランチ

M

mackerel **saba**
mandarin **mikan**
mangetout **sayaendō**
marinate (v.) *tsukeru* 漬ける, *marine suru* マリネする
marlin **kajiki**
meal **shokuji**, **gohan**
meat **niku**
milk 1. (cow's) *gyū nyū* 牛乳 2. (artificial coffee cream)
  miruku ミルク
millet 1. (barnyard) **hie** 2. (foxtail) **awa** 3. (proso) **kibi**
milt **shirako**
mince (n.) *hiki niku* 挽き肉
monosodium glutamate *gurutaminsan natoriumu* グルタミン酸ナ
  トリウム, (chemical seasoning) *kagaku chōmiryō* 化学調味料
mortar **usu**
MSG *See* monosodium glutamate.
mugwort **yomogi**
mullet **bora**
mung bean **ryokutō**
mushroom **kinoko**
mussel **igai**, *mūrugai* ムール貝
mustard **karashi**

N

noodles **menrui** 麺類
nutmeg *natsumegu* ナツメグ, *nikuzuku* にくずく

O

oats *ōtomugi* オート麦, *enbaku* えんばく 燕麦, *karasumugi* から
　すむぎ 烏麦

octopus **tako**

offal **motsu**

oil *abura* 油

oily *aburakkoi* 油っこい

onion **tamanegi**

oyster **kaki 1**

P

parch *iru* 煎る

peach *momo* 桃

pear 1. (Japanese) **nashi**　2. (Western) *seiyōnashi*　西洋梨

peas **endō**

pepper **koshō**

perilla **shiso**

persimmon **kaki 2**

pestle **kine**

pheasant **kiji**

pickle **tsukemono**

pike **kamasu**

pine nut *matsu no mi* まつのみ　松の実

plate **sara**

plum *sumomo* すもも 李, *puramu* プラム

pollack **suketōdara**

pomegranate *zakuro* ざくろ　石榴, 柘榴

pomelo **buntan**

pomfret **managatsuo**

poppy seed **keshinomi**

pork **buta niku**

pot **nabe**

potato **jagaimo**, **bareisho**

prawn **ebi**

preservative *bōfuzai* 防腐剤, *hozonryō* 保存料

preserve (n.) *hozon shokuhin* 保存食品. *See also* **tsukudani**.

puffer **fugu**

pumpkin **kabocha**

Q

quail **uzura**

quail's egg *uzura no tamago* 鶉の卵

quince 1. (European or Middle Eastern) **marumero** 2. (Chinese)
  karin

R

radish 1. (giant white) **daikon** 2. (small red) *radisshu* ラディッ
  シュ, *hatsuka daikon* 二十日大根

rainbow trout **nijimasu**

rape **aburana**

rapeseed oil *natane abura* 菜種油

rape shoot **nanohana**

raspberry *ki ichigo* きいちご 木苺

ray **ei**

rice 1. (growing) *ine* 稲 2. (harvested but uncooked) **kome**
  3. (cooked) **meshi**, **gohan**

rice ball **musubi**, **o-nigiri**

rice bran *nuka* 糠

rice flour *komeko*. The three kinds usually available are 1. non-
  glutinous rice flour *jōshinko* 上糝粉, 上新粉 2. glutinous rice
  flour *mochigomeko* 糯米粉 3. a mixture of 1 and 2 for making
  dango

rice gruel 1. (plain or with **umeboshi**) **kayu** 2. (with fish or fowl and vegetables) **zōsui**, **o-jiya**

rice vinegar *komesu* 米酢

rice wine **sake 1**, *seishu* 清酒, **nihonshu**

rich *koku ga aru* こくがある

ripe *jukushita* じゅくした　熟した

rockfish **mebaru**

roe *ko* 子

rye *raimugi* ライ麦

rye flour *raimugiko* ライ麦粉

S

salmon **sake 2** (also pronounced *shake*)

salmon roe 1. (separated eggs) **ikura** 2. (in the sac) **sujiko**

salt **shio**

sardine **iwashi**

sauce 1. (especially for *yakimono*) **tare** 2. (Worcester and the like) **sōsu**, **usutā sōsu**

saury **sanma**

scale (fish) *uroko* うろこ

scallion **rakkyō**

scallop **hotategai**. (The adductor muscle **kaibashira** of other shellfish closely resembles a scallop without its beard.)

scraper *sukurēpā* スクレーパー, *gomubera* ゴムベラ

sea bass **suzuki**

sea bream **tai**

sea cucumber **namako**

sea pike **kamasu**

sea slug **namako**

sea squirt **hoya**

sea urchin **uni**

seaweed **kaisō**

seed *tane* 種

sesame **goma**

Seville orange **daidai**

shad **konoshiro**

shaddock **buntan**

shallow-fry *itameru* 炒める

shark 1. (in general) **same** 2. (some of the larger sharks) **fuka**

shaved ice *kakigōri* かき氷. Fruit syrup is poured on top of a
bowl of shaved ice as a refreshing summer snack.

shell *kara* 殻

shellfish *kai* 貝

shoot **moyashi**

shrimp **ebi**

sieve **koshiki**, **uragoshi**

simmer **niru**

skate **ei**

skewer **kushi**

skipjack **katsuo**

smelt **wakasagi**

smoke (v.) *kunsei ni suru* 薫製にする, 燻製にする

snack 1. (afternoon tea, light refreshment) **o-yatsu** 2. (light
meal) *keishoku* 軽食

snap bean **sayaingen**

snow crab **zuwaigani**

snow pea **sayaendō**

soda water *tansansui* 炭酸水, *sōda uōtā* ソーダウォーター

sodium bicarbonate *jūtansan natoriumu* 重炭酸ナトリウム

sole **shitabirame**

soybean **daizu**

soy milk *tōnyū* 豆乳

soy sauce **shōyu**

Spanish mackerel **sawara**

sparrow **suzume**

spice **kōshinryō**, *supaisu* スパイス

spinach **hōrensō**

spiny lobster **ise ebi**

spoon (china) **renge**, **chirirenge**

spring onion **wakegi**

spring roll *harumaki* 春巻き

squash **kabocha**

squid **ika**

starch **denpun**

steam (v.) *musu* 蒸す

steamer 1. (metal) **mushiki** 2. (wood or bamboo) **seirō**

sticky rice **mochigome**

stingray **ei**

stir-fry (v.) *itameru* 炒める

stock **dashi**, **dashijiru**

strawberry **ichigo**

sugar **satō**

sugar pea **sayaendō**

supper *yūshoku* 夕食

sweet (adj.) *amai* 甘い

sweetmeat **kashi**

sweet pepper **piiman**

sweet potato **satsumaimo**

swordfish **kajiki**

T

tangerine **mikan**

taro **satoimo**

tea 1. (green) **o-cha** (or **cha**) 2. (powdered) **matcha** 3. (Western) *kōcha* 紅茶

teapot 1. (with bamboo handle) **dobin** 2. (with pottery lug for handle) **kyūsu**

tempura flour *tempura ko* 天ぷら粉

thickener *koku suru mono* 濃くするもの, *toromi o tuskeru mono* とろみをつけるもの, e.g., **kuzu** and **katakuriko**

threadsail fish **kawahagi**

tilefish   **amadai**

tongue   *tan* タン

topping   **furikake**, *toppingu* トッピング

top-shell   **sazae**

trefoil   **mitsuba**

trout   1. (brook) **kawamasu**   2. (rainbow) **nijimasu**

tuna, tunny   **maguro**

turbo   **sazae**

turnip   **kabu**

turtle (soft-shelled)   **suppon**

U

unpolished rice   **genmai**

unsalted butter   *muen batā* 無塩バター

V

variety meat   **motsu**

veal   *ko ushi no niku* 仔牛の肉, 犢

vegetable   **yasai**

vegetable oil   *shokubutsu yushi* 植物油脂

vegetarianism   *saishokushugi* 菜食主義

venison   *shika niku* 鹿肉

Venus clam   **hamaguri**

vinegar   **su**

W

walnut   **kurumi**

water   1. (cold) *mizu* 水   2. (hot) *yu* ゆ 湯   3. (boiling) *futtō shiteiru o-yu* 沸騰しているお湯, *nettō* 熱湯

water caltrop   **hishinomi**

water chestnut   **hishinomi**
watercress   *kureson* クレソン
watermelon   **suika**
welsh onion   **negi**
whale   **kujira**
wheat flour   *komugiko* 小麦粉
whelk   1. (*Babylonia japonica*) **bai**   2. (*Neptunea arthritica*)
  tsubu
whitebait   **shirauo**
whiting   **kisu**
whole-wheat flour   *zenryūfun* 全粒粉
wild boar   *See* boar.
Worcester sauce   **usutā sōsu**, **sōsu**
wrasse   **bera**

Y

yam   **yamanoimo**, **yamaimo**
yellowfin tuna   **kihada**
yellowtail   1. (adult) **buri**   2. (young) **hamachi**, **inada**
yolk   *kimi* 黄身

Z

zest (of citrus fruits)   *kawa* 皮

Appendices

1. Chopsticks   183

2. Katsuobushi   185

3. The Kitchen and Its Utensils   187

4. Kombu   190

5. The Meal   193

6. Miso   196

7. Saké   198

8. Salt   200

9. Sansai   202

10. Soy Sauce   204

11. Sushi   206

12. Tea   208

13. The Tea Ceremony   210

14. Umami and Flavor   211

15. Vegetarianism   216

16. Wasabi   218

17. Wasanbon Sugar   219

蒸
し
て
ろ
乾
と
奥
だ
る
制
を

The above illustration, taken from *Nihon sankai meisan zue*, published in Osaka in 1799, shows the making of *katsuobushi*.

1 ❖ Chopsticks

The Japanese have not always eaten with chopsticks (**hashi**). Until the end of the eighth century the common people ate with their hands. The nobility had already started using chopsticks and spoon after the Chinese fashion, but the spoon was never taken up by the common people and by the tenth century had gone out of use among the nobility.

Compared with the flat-ended Chinese chopsticks, the Japanese ones are rather short. On average, Chinese chopsticks are 26 cm long, whereas the Japanese ones for home use are about 22 cm and the Korean ones even shorter at 19 cm. However, different kinds of chopsticks are used for different purposes and some of these are very short.

At home, chopsticks for eating are usually made of lacquered wood or bamboo, and superior ones are, or rather were, made of ivory. On special occasions such as New Year, high-quality plain wood disposable chopsticks are used, folded up in a piece of paper called *hashi-gami*. On such occasions a chopstick rest (*hashioki*) might be used, but many people don't even possess chopstick rests, let alone use them.

In the kitchen, **saibashi** of various sizes are used for cooking and for other purposes, such as getting things out of bottles. Such chopsticks are extremely convenient.

Notes: Boldface indicates an entry in the Japanese-English section.

Out-of-doors, **waribashi** are the rule. These are disposable chopsticks and are made as a pair in one piece, prepared so as to be pulled apart into separate sticks at the time of use. It is quite obvious that they have never been used. They usually come in a little paper envelope called *hashibukuro*. Being disposable, they save restaurants a lot of washing up, but do seem to be rather wasteful. It is estimated that eight billion of them are used in a year. From the point of view of a foreigner not entirely at ease with chopsticks, *waribashi* are wretched. They always break apart the wrong way, sometimes so much so that you have the embarrassment of asking for another pair. And being much shorter than ordinary chopsticks, they are difficult for people with large hands to manage. The only way to avoid problems with *waribashi* is to carry your own chopsticks, a custom that might well be encouraged.

Prawns served in the shell, whether to save trouble or more likely because they are more decorative that way, cannot be peeled with chopsticks. A lot of people abandon them, but some brave souls revert to the ancient custom of eating with the fingers, or they peel them with their fingers and put them into their mouth with chopsticks.

Chopsticks clearly determine the way food must be served. Food has to be served in pieces that are manageable, though the limits often seem to be stretched with **furai**, especially the very popular *ebi furai*, large prawns deep-fried in a coating of egg and bread crumbs, which might be big enough for about three mouthfuls.

Finally, chopsticks are the ultimate criterion of whether or not a food can be considered Japanese. If a food can neither be drunk from a bowl, nor eaten with chopsticks, then it is not considered Japanese. For example, *pōku katsu* (pork cutlet) is the same as **tonkatsu**, except that it is left in the piece and has to be eaten with knife and fork. It is therefore not Japanese. Neither is curry and rice (*karē raisu*), since it is eaten with a spoon.

2 ✦ Katsuobushi

Smoked, dried bonito (**katsuobushi**) is such an essential, everyday product that there is no general awareness of just how remarkable it is. It is for all the world like a moldy chunk of wood, and to prepare it for use it is actually shaved on the kitchen equivalent of a carpenter's plane. In fact, the language of *katsuobushi* is the language of wood. *Bushi* means a lump or knot of wood and the best *katsuobushi* (in the piece) is referred to as *hon kare bushi*, *kare* meaning seasoned (of wood). The shavings are used to make the standard stock for soups and dips (**dashi**). *Katsuobushi* itself is quite unique to Japan, made by a complicated process, apparently without an equivalent anywhere else in the world, which was perfected about 1675 in the district of Kishu, southeast of Osaka. Prior to that, the bonito (**katsuo**) was simply dried, without the smoking and curing that the perfected process requires.

The process begins, of course, with the catching of the fish, which in itself is a remarkable feat. The fishermen are ranged fairly close to each other along the gunwales of the fishing boat, casting their lines with unbaited hook and landing their catches with a rapidity that has to be seen to be believed and a dexterity that miraculously keeps their neighbors from having their eyes fetched out. Most of the fish are brought in fresh either to Makurazaki, at the southeastern tip of Kyushu, or to Tosa, on the southern coast of Shikoku. It is in these two places that most *katsuobushi* is nowadays made.

As soon as the fish are landed, the unique process, which is beautifully shown in outline in a series of illustrations in *Nihon sankai meisan zue*, published in 1799, begins. (*See* p. 182.) First of all, the fish, which can weigh up to 4.5 kilograms, are filleted into two, and then the fillets from the larger fish are halved, a process known as *namagiri*. The fish is then simmered for twenty minutes to set the protein, which comprises 77% of the dry matter. This process is called *nijuku*. An hour later, the bones are removed with tweezers (**hone nuki**).

The smoking process (*mizunuki baikan*, meaning dry heating) is the next stage. For six or more hours a day everyday for up to two weeks, the fish is hot-smoked in a chamber with the smoke of various oaks, or sometimes wild cherry, beech, or chestnut. This process reduces the moisture content of the fish, which is now called *arabushi*, coarse fillets, from 70% to 25%. These are trimmed and put out in the sun for two or three days to dry and are called *hadaka-bushi*, naked fillets.

Next begins the long process of curing (*kabizuke*), which will remove the remaining moisture. The trays of *hadakabushi* are placed in a chamber impregnated with the mold *Aspergillus glaucus*. Long-established mold chambers have no need for the mold to be introduced, since it is already there in abundance. After two weeks, the fillets with the first growth of mold are removed from the chamber and placed out-of-doors for the sun to kill off the surface mold, a process known as *hiboshi*. The molding and sunning are repeated over a period of six weeks until the fillets become like completely dried-out chunks of wood. The sound given out when you tap one piece against another indicates the quality. The higher the note the better. *Katsuobushi* in this form will keep forever.

The fillets of *katsuobushi* must be shaved for use. *Katsuobushi* planes are identical with carpenter's planes except that they are mounted upside-down on a box with a drawer for the shavings to drop into. The box with plane is called simply *katsuobushi bako*, literally *katsuobushi* box. Machines do the job commercially. It is the shavings (**kezuribushi**) that are used in cooking. Nowadays few households and only the best restaurants shave the *katsuobushi* in the traditional way, yet the *katsuobushi bako* is still sometimes given as a traditional wedding gift.

Unique as the making of *katsuobushi* is, the shavings are not something out of the ordinary. One way or another, they are necessary in the preparation of every Japanese meal. Ideally the shavings are made at the time of cooking, and it is said that high-class restaurants wait until the customer appears before shaving the *katsuobushi* for his soup stock. The best of the fragrance is very volatile and soon decreases. Shaving the *katsuobushi* on a plane at home used to be the norm, but nowadays most people buy bags of shavings at the supermarket. All that can be said for store-bought shavings is that they are convenient. The fragrance cannot compare with that of the freshly shaved shavings.

The best **dashi** is made by immersing *katsuobushi* shavings in boiling water for a short time and then straining off the liquid. When well made, this *dashi* (*katsuodashi*) has an incomparable aroma and goes particularly well with the sliver of citron peel (**yuzu**) in Japanese consomme (**suimono**). The dipping sauce for tempura (**tentsuyu**) is also based on stock made with *katsuodashi*.

Katsuobushi shavings are also used as a relish, for example, sprinkled on top of cold tofu. They provide sodium inosinate, a nucleotide that increases the **umami** (for which *see also* Appendix 14), that is to say, it boosts the flavor.

3 ✦ The Kitchen and Its Utensils

In Japanese advertisements for "mansions" (flats, apartments) the letters LDK, standing for Living, Dining, Kitchen, are often seen. Since LDK has an interesting connection with the traditional Japanese kitchen, I shall start by describing that room.

The Traditional Kitchen

The part of a traditional Japanese house set aside for cooking and eating, though considered to be one area, was in two parts. The first part, *doma*, was at ground level and indeed often simply had the beaten earth of the ground as floor. This was where the **kamado** stood, at which rice and miso soup were cooked. The *nagashidai* was also here, for cleaning vegetables and washing dishes and utensils, always in cold water. Cold water, considered purer than hot water, was sufficient, since nothing was greasy or oily. The windows did not let in a great deal of light, since they were fitted with vertical slats and horizontal shelves on which the cooking utensils were ranged. Smoke escaped as best it could without a flue.

The second part was adjacent to the *doma*, but at the raised level of the rest of the house. Though under the same section of the roof as the lower part, this was the living and dining area and contained the **irori** (centrally situated hearth), sunk in the middle of wooden flooring, where that was the custom. City houses did not have *irori*, nor was it customary in western Japan. Although the primary purpose of the *irori* was for heating, certain kinds of cooking, such as **o-yaki** and **kiri-tanpo**, could be done there, and possibly even certain **nabemono** with the *jizaikagi*, a hook suspended from the rafters, on which to hang the pot. This hook was normally used for the kettle to heat water for tea. Above the *irori* was a shelf called *hidana* or *hodana*, which could be used for smoking food, since there was no flue. The smoke from the fire found its own way out, killing off unwanted mosquitoes and other insects in the process.

These two adjacent parts of the traditional kitchen were treated as a single living-dining-kitchen area, an early version of today's LDK, which in turn leads us to the modern kitchen (**daidokoro**).

The Modern Kitchen

Whereas modern houses generally have a separate kitchen (still with shelves placed in the windows for storing utensils), in apartments the kitchen, dining, and living areas tend to overlap in the LDK pattern, thus continuing the layout of the traditional house. Although kitchens are provided with water heaters, some people still prefer to wash the dishes in cold water. Cooking is normally done on two gas rings, since ovens are not used in Japanese cooking, though nowadays microwave ovens are almost universal and sometimes also operate as regular ovens for cooking Western food, which is very popular. Many people love to bake cakes, cookies, and even bread. Frozen foods are slowly becoming more accepted and the microwave is useful for preparing these, as is also the popular oven toaster, in which, also, the toast for a Western-style breakfast, now more common than the traditional Japanese breakfast, can be made. The working area in the kitchen is always minimal.

The *kamado*, that important symbol of traditional family unity, has been replaced by the automatic rice cooker; the **seirō** (traditional wooden steamer) has been replaced by the **mushiki** (modern-style aluminum steamer) on the gas ring, and miso soup is also made on the gas ring. In other words, apart from the rice cooker, the traditional *kamado* and **shichirin** (brazier) have both been replaced by the gas **konro**. There are usually only two rings, an arrangement that is quite limiting for Western cookery, as is the cramped work space. People from Western countries usually find Japanese kitchens rather hard to adapt to.

Utensils

Pots, pans, plates, bowls, and ladles are much the same everywhere. But the Japanese kitchen has a number of utensils that are very interesting and quite unique. The following utensils are described in the Japanese-English section of the dictionary: **dobin** (teapot); **hōchō** (knife); **hone nuki** (fish-bone tweezers); **ichimonji** (scraper-spatula); **kamado** (kitchen range); **katsuobushi bako** (box for shaving *katsuobushi*); **komebitsu** (rice chest); **koshiki** (sieve); **kyūsu** (small teapot); **makisu** (mat for sushi); **manaita** (chopping board); **menbō** (rolling pin); **nabe** (pot, saucepan); **nuki'ita** (type of board); **o-hitsu** (container for serving rice); **oroshigane** (grater); **otoshibuta** (drop-lid); **renge** (Chinese spoon); **saibashi** (kitchen chopsticks); **sasara** (brush); **shichirin** (brazier); **suihanki** (automatic rice cooker); **suribachi** (mortar); **surikogi** (pestle); **tamajakushi** (ladle); **tawashi** (brush); **teppan** (hot plate); **toishi** (whetstone); **zaru** (colander).

Usu and **kine** (the large mortar and pestle) were not used in the kitchen, but in an area just outside the kitchen. Sometimes they were operated by foot-power.

The following are dining rather than kitchen equipment: **chabu-dai** (low table); **jūbako** (tiered food box); **oshiki** (dining tray); **zen** (individual low table).

Some of these utensils and pieces of equipment are not only useful but most unusual. The *katsuobushi bako* is quite unique to Japan. The whole idea of making stock with shavings of cured fish is imaginative, to say the least. Then to bring the carpenter's plane into the kitchen to make the shavings can only increase the unusualness of this operation. The blade must be very sharp and very finely adjusted, or else the *katsuobushi* comes out as a powder.

The mortar and pestle known as *suribachi* and *surikogi* too are unusual and extremely useful, as anyone who has tried to bray sesame in a smooth-sided mortar will attest. This type of mortar and pestle could be useful in a kitchen anywhere, not just in Japan.

The *oroshigane*, especially in its domestic ceramic form, is just as useful for grating apple as it is for **daikon**. All shapes and sizes are available, and often both shape and glaze are very beautiful. The same can be said of pottery storage-jars (*kame* 瓶, 甕) with their pattern of glaze dripping down from the rim.

Finally, the Japanese steamer (*kaku seirō*) is not only beautiful but very practical. Unfortunately it is also rather expensive and not easy to get hold of. (*See also* **seirō**.)

The traditional Japanese cooking utensils bring art and craftsmanship into the kitchen and comprise a unique and very practical *batterie de cuisine*.

4 ❖ Kombu

The Japanese are great eaters of seaweed. The coastal waters provide many different kinds in abundance. Seaweed is easily preserved by drying, is easily transported, has an indefinite shelf life, is highly nutritious, and can be prepared and served in many tasty ways.

"Tasty" is a very significant word, since it was in Japan that the importance of monosodium glutamate with regard to taste was discovered, researched, and promoted through the concept of **umami**. (*See also* Appendix 14.) Monosodium glutamate was discovered in the remains of some stock a scientist had accidentally boiled dry during his researches in flavor and nutrition. The stock was made of the seaweed known as kelp or tangle or kombu, **konbu** in Japanese and botanically known as *Laminaria*. There are more than ten species of kombu used for food in Japan, the commonest being *Laminaria japonica*. It is the best-known dietary source of iodine and a rich source of iron and other minerals as well as vitamin B1.

Kombu grows in the cold waters off the coast of northern Japan, mostly around the northern part of Hokkaido. If the water gets too warm for too long (longer than a couple of months at 20°C or more), the kombu dies. New growth is not from the stem, but from the tip of the leaf, and it is the second- or third-year growths that are harvested, since they are the best for food. Harvesting is done with long poles with forks or hooks at the end, from July to September. Specially constructed kombu boats take the harvesters out to the kombu beds. Only kombu harvested live from the sea is eaten, dead fronds washed up on the shore not being so flavorful.

Once brought to land by the boats, the kombu is spread out on the ground to dry in the sun. Nowadays the drying-off process is completed by hot-air fans in drying chambers. The kombu is then folded, made up into bundles, and sent to market.

The most basic form of kombu on the market is *dashikonbu*, fairly large pieces of blade kombu used for making stock. This kombu should not be washed but at most should only be wiped with a slightly damp cloth. This is because the flavor lies on the surface, which also means that the kombu should be left in the boiling water only for a short time, ten minutes or twelve at the most.

Although stock made from **katsuobushi** is much more fragrant than that made from kombu, kombu contributes greatly as a flavor enhancer because of the very high amount of natural monosodium glutamate it provides. It became important for stock making because of the Buddhist rejection of the eating of any kind of flesh. Thus, from early times Kyoto, the center of Buddhist vegetarianism, and its neighboring port Osaka became the main centers of kombu distribution and use. Kyoto cooking still places great emphasis on the use of kombu in many different ways.

Kombu appears in many guises. It starts off a dark brown-green color and when dried, of course, is even darker. Seaweed shops sell dried blades over a meter in length, but usually it is packaged in shorter pieces, the width normally being about 10 cm. Also sold are very small pieces for sucking (*o-shaburi konbu*, for which *see also* **konbu**).

Kombu is shaved in various ways, often after being soaked in vinegar and dried again. This is **oboro konbu** or **tororo konbu**. There is also *kizami konbu*, an aristocratic exotic product traditionally favored by imperial nuns. This, like other forms of kombu, is sometimes served deep-fried.

Another way of preparing kombu is to boil it with soy sauce in the preparation called *tsukudani konbu*. Cut into small squares, this is much used as **tsumamimono** to go with drinks.

Kombu suitably prepared is also used for rolling up various fillings such as sardines. The rolls can be served on their own or put with many other ingredients into the hot stock of a popular dish known as **o-den**, which is always served with very hot mustard.

Last but not least there is kombu tea (*kobucha*). Powdered kombu and sometimes other dried ingredients such as perilla (**shiso**) and Japanese apricot (**ume**), with a little salt, are mixed with boiling water and drunk as a kind of herb tea. It makes a tasty, nutritious, caffeine-free drink. Not surprisingly, the best of these teas come from Kyoto.

Kombu is said to be good for reducing high blood pressure, and many people drink the water in which a piece of the root end of a kombu blade has been soaked overnight as a medicine.

Finally, there is the ritual use of kombu. It forms part of the special New Year decorations in the home and is often used as a food gift to the gods in Shinto shrines.

5 ✦ The Meal

Meals vary according to the needs of the occasion, and appropriate styles develop. The main styles of meal in Japan are the family meal, the packed meal, and the formal meal.

The Family Meal

Ordinary people in Japan started using tables only in the second half of last century. Until then, individual settings of food were served on trays (**oshiki**) or trays with legs (**zen**) in front of each person on the floor. This custom has by no means died out and has at any rate ensured, in contrast to the Chinese custom, that food is normally served in individual portions. The main exceptions to this are communal one-pot dishes such as sukiyaki, cooked at table, and the special New Year **o-sechi ryōri**, which is packed in one set of boxes for all. At a family meal, all the dishes except those that really need to be eaten hot (rice and soup) are placed on the table beforehand, normally in individual portions. The main exception might be pickles. Since some people like to eat a lot of them and others don't like them at all, it is more practical to have pickles on a communal plate. Few housewives spend the day considering the aesthetics of arranging three sardines on a plate as a professional chef might do, so the appearance of the food on the table is attractive rather than aesthetically captivating.

The menu is normally the basic **ichijū sansai** (a soup and three dishes), followed by (or with) rice, pickles, and tea. The three dishes are usually **namasu** (sashimi or vinegared raw fish), **nimono** (a gently simmered dish), and **yakimono** (a grilled dish). These three could be replaced by **nabemono** (a one-pot dish). Fresh fruit is often served right at the end of the meal with the tea.

The Packed Meal

The boxed meal (**bentō**) is an excellent and highly adaptable institution. Anything from a simple school lunch or a picnic or a lunch on the train to the *haute cuisine* of the *shōkadō bentō* or the somewhat less grand **makunouchi bentō** (originally designed for eating during the interval of a Kabuki performance) can be packed in a box and taken wherever it is needed. It doesn't necessarily have to be taken anywhere. There are restaurants, especially in Kyoto, which specialize in **bentō** meals. In this case, all the food may not be contained in the box, which is but the centerpiece of an exquisite still life. Only hunger could prompt one to disturb the tastefully arranged morsels.

The overriding consideration in making a **bentō** is to have a variety of different-colored foods and to arrange them in an aesthetically pleasing way. There should be at least ten different items, though the **shōjin ryōri** vegetarian **bentō** sold on Kyoto Station Shinkansen platforms contains over twenty items. The rice can be served in a separate box that forms a nest of two boxes. Traditionally the rice is cold, but nowadays many **bentō** takeaway shops put piping-hot rice in at the last moment.

Formal Meals

Formal meals offer the area above all for intricate rules governing appearance, since it is here that appearance is the most important thing. Ka'ichi Tsuji, one of the great masters of high-class Japanese cuisine writes, "There is nothing more important in Japanese food than arranging it well, with special regard to the color, on plates chosen to suit the food" (辻嘉一 『四季の盛りつけ料理の色と形』). The absence of any reference to flavor is revealing. Donald Richie, in his highly recommended book *A Taste of Japan*, writes, "The food is to be looked at as well as eaten. The admiration to be elicited is more, or other, than gustatory. The appeal has its own satisfactions, and it may truly be said that in Japan the eyes are at least as large as the stomachs. Certainly the number of rules involving modes and methods of presentation indicate the importance of eye appeal."

There are two main types of formal meal. Firstly, there is the meal that you would typically get at a wedding reception. Here, as much of the food as possible is laid on the table beforehand. Things like soup and hot savory custard are served during the meal. Sushi or **sekihan** (glutinous rice steamed with adzuki beans, a celebratory and most delicious dish) might be served at the end of the meal, not so much with the intention that the guests should eat it then and there, but that they should take it home.

The menu would be composed on the following basis: **zensai** (appetizers); **suimono** (clear soup); sashimi (raw fish); **yakimono** (grilled food); **mushimono** (steamed food); **nimono** (simmered food); **age-mono** (deep-fried food); **sunomono** (vinegared foods) or **aemono** (cooked salad).

The end of the meal is more variable, but as mentioned above, *sekihan* is likely to be served. Fresh fruit and tea will very likely also be served.

The second type of formal meal is known as **kaiseki ryōri**. (*Ryōri* means cookery, food, cuisine.) Actually there are two kinds of *kaiseki*, indicated by two different ways of writing the expression. The formal kind is designed to be served at a full tea ceremony and hence is called **cha kaiseki**. The other *kaiseki* tends to be a rather jovial drinking party.

In all the formal meals the diner is given no choice. The chef decides the menu, which he does according to strict and elaborate rules, the first of which is that the menu must highlight the season. Then plates and vessels must be chosen to suit the food. The basic rule is that round pieces of food should be placed on a square dish and square or long-shaped pieces of food must be put on a round dish. One needs a lot of dishes, since the pattern and color of the dish should also suit the season. The food is arranged on the dish according to the Japanese rules of **moritsuke**.

Of course, there are many other kinds of meal to suit different occasions. A traditional Japanese breakfast follows the basic pattern of rice, miso soup, pickles, and side dishes. Picnics, often with a widely varied menu, are also popular.

6 ❖ Miso

Miso is a fermented paste of grain and soybeans. It is not only a highly nutritious basic Japanese foodstuff, but also has many uses as a very savory flavoring. There are innumerable varieties, but the basic categories are rice miso, made from rice, soybeans, and salt; barley miso, made from barley, soybeans, and salt; and soybean miso, with only soybeans and salt. Western Japan favors barley miso and sweet rice miso; a fairly restricted area of central Japan favors soybean miso (**hatchō miso**); and the rest of the country, rather salty rice miso, which represents over 80% of the miso sold in Japan. Red miso (**akamiso**), which comprises about 75% of all rice miso, is red to brown in color and high in protein and salt. White miso (**shiromiso**), by contrast, is rather sweet. It is a famous product of Kyoto, expensive and regarded as high class. It is particularly useful in **aemono** and in sweets. There are also variety misos, usually eaten as a relish rather than used as an ingredient, and which are often quite sweet and contain vegetables as well as whole soybeans, or flavorings such as **yuzu** (Japanese citron) or mustard.

To make miso, rice or barley that has been steamed is allowed to cool almost to body temperature and is inoculated with spores of the *Aspergillus oryzae* mold and cultured for a couple of days. Then soybeans are washed, cooked, cooled, crushed, and mixed with the cultured rice or barley **kōji** along with salt and water. This mash is put into 2-m deep cedar vats and the slow process of fermentation begins. For the best miso this would see two summers, during which period bacteria and enzymes transform the grain and beans into a highly nutritious paste, deep in color and rich in aroma. It consists of about 14% high-quality protein and has a consistency similar to peanut butter. The color ranges from very dark brown to yellow, and the salt content ranges from 5% to 15%.

The early history of miso in Japan is not at all clear. Miso derives from the Chinese *chiang* and it could be that two different traditions, one coming via Korea and the other direct from China, have evolved the same product by slightly different methods. The arrival in Japan would have been during the sixth or seventh century. Before that, the Japanese used **hishio**, mainly fish products such as **shiokara** and **uoshōyu**, a fish sauce similar to those of Southeast Asia.

In the year 701, Emperor Mommu established a bureau to regulate the production, trade, and taxation of miso. By this time, Japanese miso had probably acquired its own character, quite distinct from the Chinese *chiang* of its origins, and by the end of the century different Chinese characters were being used to write the name. In the early days, miso was made by Buddhist monks at the temples and was consumed especially at the imperial court. However, by the middle of the tenth century, miso was no longer restricted to the capital, but was being made in the provinces, ready for the great food revolution that was brought about by the reformist warrior government of the Kamakura period (1185–1333). Until this time, Buddhist monks had largely catered to the effete aristocrats at the imperial court in Kyoto. Now they began to concern themselves with the spiritual needs of the common people and encouraged a simple, healthy life with two vegetarian meals a day. A simple meal consisting of rice (or barley, or millet for the really poor), pickled vegetables, and miso soup became the norm and has remained so ever since. The high nutritional value of miso has been a very important feature of the Japanese diet from that time on.

Thus, miso soup, which the Chinese had never made from their *chiang*, was a Japanese product of the Kamakura period. However, it was not until the Muromachi period (1333–1568), when the government returned to Kyoto from Kamakura, that miso as such became really popular, with various culinary uses developing quite apart from soup, and different varieties of miso becoming popular in different areas.

The main types of miso have been mentioned above. There are also many "variety" misos, perhaps the best known of which is *kinzanji* miso. *Kinzanji* miso differs from other miso in being made from a special *kōji* that contains both soybeans and whole-grain barley, traditionally in equal proportions. Nowadays, however, the proportion of barley is greatly increased to give a sweeter, more easily made product. A chunky texture results not only from the presence of the whole grains of barley but also from the soybeans, which are roasted and cracked. All sorts of vegetables and seasonings are added, including chopped eggplant, ginger, burdock, white pickling melon (**shirouri**), kombu, **daikon**, and cucumber. **Shiso** leaves and seeds, **sanshō** pepper, and **tōgarashi** pepper can be added for seasoning. The fermentation period lasts for six months, and the vegetables and seasonings may be added at the start or halfway through.

Kinzan-ji is the name of one of China's five great Sung-dynasty Zen Buddhist temples, and it is thought by some that the prototype of *kinzanji* miso was brought to Japan from China in the middle of the thirteenth century. Misos of the *kinzanji* type are used as toppings for slices of crisp vegetables such as cucumber, or with rice or rice gruel, whereas regular miso is above all used for soup (**miso shiru**), in **nimono** and **yakimono** (**dengaku**), as a medium for pickling miso pickles (**misozuke**), and in many other ways.

7 ✦ Saké

Even in English, saké is the preferable name for Japanese rice "wine," since the word wine is not really appropriate, though it is true that both saké and wine are products of yeast fermentation. In Japan saké is also called **nihonshu** 日本酒 (Japanese liquor) or *sei shu* 清酒 (pure liquor).

The wealth of variety of saké available throughout Japan is quite amazing, for not only do all the big saké breweries produce a wide range of sakés to be distributed nationally, but all over the country small local breweries produce their local saké (**jizake**).

The Brewing of Saké

The brewing of saké is quite a complicated process. Winter is the best time to make it, since, among other things, the cold affords better control over the fermentation. First of all, large-grain rice of high quality is chosen and polished. Polishing is a very variable factor, depending on the type of saké to be produced. In the best *ginjōshu*, the highest quality saké, only 30% of the grain may be left, but in lesser quality saké, only 30% of the grain may be removed. After polishing, the rice is washed and soaked for a short while and then steamed.

About one-quarter of the steamed rice is used for making **kōji**, being cooled to about 30°C for the purpose; the rest, to be used in the actual fermentation, is cooled to a much lower temperature, about 5°C. Making the *kōji* takes about thirty-five hours in a special room kept hot and humid to encourage the growth of the mold *Aspergillus oryzae*, which is sprinkled over the rice. Next, the *kōji* and yeast are mixed in a tank of water, and the rest of the steamed rice is added. The yeast multiplies and fermentation begins. This is now called the seed mash (*moto*). When the seed mash has matured, it is transferred to the fermentation tank, where fermentation continues for about three months, with *kōji*, water, and steamed rice being added at three intervals. During this period, the *kōji* converts the rice starch into sugars, and the yeast simultaneously starts the alcohol fermentation. This is what is called **moromi** (the main mash). When fermentation is complete, the *moromi* is pressed through cloth under high pressure and the residual lees (**sakekasu**) formed into blocks to be used for cooking and pickling. The slight cloudiness left in the saké is removed either by filtration or simply by allowing it to settle. The saké is then pasteurized at 60°C and stored in tanks to mature for several months. It is then blended and bottled.

Types of Saké

There are many different kinds of saké. *Ginjōshu*, the ultimate of the saké brewer's art, has been mentioned above. It is expensive and hard to get, being made in very limited quantities. The very best never reaches the market.

Saké usually has rectified alcohol added, but there is no added alcohol in *junmaishu* (pure rice saké). It is consequently fairly heavy.

Honjōzukuri is a saké that has a rich, traditional flavor but at the same time has a much appreciated mildness. Added alcohol must not exceed 25% of the total alcohol. *Ginjōshu* is the top grade of *honjōzukuri*.

Nigorizake is cloudy because the cloth through which it is filtered is not tightly woven. It is similar to **doburoku** (illegal home-brewed saké) and may be unpasteurized, in which case it is "alive" and still fermenting.

Sweet and Dry

Saké ranges from bone dry to fairly sweet. Dry is *karakuchi* 辛口 and sweet is *amakuchi* 甘口. There is an official scale of sweetness and dryness, the *nihonshu do*, running from -10 to +10. ±0 is neutral, +10 is quite dry, and -10 is quite sweet, but other factors, especially acidity, affect the individual perception of sweetness and dryness. The only way, ultimately, to find out about saké is to engage in some serious tasting.

8 ❖ Salt

There are no salt deposits anywhere in Japan so all salt (**shio**) has either to be taken from the sea or imported. The importation of salt, now on a considerable scale for industrial use, is a comparatively recent development, and in the not too distant past, all salt used in Japan was extracted from the sea locally. All ordinary table salt still is. It is one of the ironies of marketing that many people seek out the more expensive salt labeled sea salt, apparently unaware that such specialty salt is more likely to contain added non-sea salt from foreign salt deposits.

Japan is too humid for natural solar evaporation in salt pans to be effective, and considerable effort and ingenuity are required to extract this basic essential from sea water. From the earliest times until about the sixth century and even later, seaweed was burnt and brine was made from the ashes. This brine was then evaporated by boiling until salt crystals formed. It wasn't until the Edo period (from the beginning of the seventeenth century) that much more effective methods of salt extraction were invented, and a huge, bustling industry, covering extensive tracts of Japan's coastline and lasting until the early 1970s, developed, especially round the coast of the Inland Sea. Here big differences in sea level between high tide and low tide enabled the flooding of tidal sand terraces to provide a more concentrated brine for further evaporation by boiling in pans until the salt crystallized out. Recently there has been a surge of interest in the salt terraces (*enden*), and Shikoku has seen a small resurgence of the type of salt terrace which superseded the tidal terrace. In this kind of salt bed the sea water is first concentrated on a sloping sand terrace, then the resulting brine is cascaded down vertical evaporation racks, with the wind assisting in evaporation. However, to help the process along, salt imported from the huge salt beds of the Western Australian desert is added nowadays at the first stage of concentration.

In other parts of Japan the work was much more laborious because buckets of sea water had to be carried to sand terraces above the tidal line. This is still done at Suzu, on the Noto Peninsula, kept going as a registered Intangible Cultural Property, and the salt thus made is available in small quantities.

Since 1972 the Japanese have extracted salt from the sea by the ion-exchange system, a process of electrolysis. The salt terraces have all but disappeared and so has the old-fashioned kind of salt that contained **nigari** (bittern), the traditional coagulant used in making bean curd. It has not disappeared entirely, however, for the old-style salt is necessary for making the pyramid-shaped bricks of salt set before the gods. The Grand Shrine of Ise, Japan's premier Shinto shrine, has its own private salt terrace, *mi-shio hama*, where salt for the ritual uses of the shrine is still made in the traditional way. Bean curd, which was traditionally curdled with *nigari*, is now mostly curdled with chemicals.

Salt is not much used at table in Japan. It is sometimes used with tempura and other deep-fried foods, as well as with **yakitori**. Yet there is no lack of salt in the ordinary Japanese meal. Far from it. There has traditionally been too much. Miso and soy sauce, both common ingredients in Japanese cooking, contain a lot of salt, and pickles, appearing at every meal, require a lot of salt in the making. Salt is also a common seasoning in cooking, often in combination with monosodium glutamate, which in any case occurs naturally in so many foods. **Shioyaki**, an excellent method of grilling fish, uses lots of salt on the fish, especially on the fins and tail, to avoid charring.

Finally, two of salt's most ancient uses in Japan are the ritual ones of purification and protecting from evil. These are seen at Shinto shrines and in the liberal scattering of salt during bouts of sumo. Little piles of salt (**morijio**) are also sometimes placed at the entrance of bars in the entertainment districts. This practice derives from an ancient Chinese custom of proprietors' putting little piles of salt outside their establishments to induce carriage oxen to stop there and lick it.

9 ❖ Sansai

The following is a list of the commonest plants used in **sansai ryōri**. The most important ones have an asterisk, referring to an entry in the Japanese-English section of the dictionary:

akaza あかざ　藜　goose foot, lamb's quarters *Chenopodium album* var. *centrorubrum*

asatsuki* あさつき　浅葱　asatsuki chive *Allium ledebourianum*

ashitaba あしたば　明日葉　angelica *Angelica keiskei*

fukinotō* ふきのとう　蕗の薹　unopened bud of Japanese butterbur *Petasites japonicus*

gyōja ninniku ぎょうじゃにんにく　行者葫　a kind of chive *Allium victorialis* var. *platyphyllum*

itadori* いたどり　虎杖　Japanese knotweed, flowering bamboo *Polygonum cuspidatum*

junsai* じゅんさい　蓴菜　water shield *Brasenia schreberi*

kanzō かんぞう　甘草　licorice *Glycyrrhiza uralensis*

katakuri* かたくり　片栗　dog's tooth violet *Erythronium japonicum*

kogomi こごみ　屈み　fiddlehead of the ostrich fern **kusasotetsu**

kusasotetsu くさそてつ　草蘇鉄　ostrich fern *Matteuccia struthiopteris*. Also called **kogomi** こごみ　屈み. The young fronds are fiddleheads.

momijigasa もみじがさ　紅葉笠　a kind of Indian plantain *Parasenecio delphiniifolia* (formerly *Cacalia delphiniifolia*). Closely related to **yobusumasō**.

nemagaritake ねまがりたけ　根曲がり竹　Chishima sasa *Sasa kurilensis*. Also called **chishimazasa** ちしまざさ　千島笹.

nobiru* のびる　野蒜　red garlic *Allium gravi*

ōbagibōshi おうばぎぼうし　大葉擬宝珠　plantain lily *Hosta sieboldiana*

okahijiki おかひじき　陸鹿尾菜　saltwort *Salsola komarovii*

sasa* ささ　笹　bamboo grass *Sasa* spp. *See also* **nemagaritake**.

seri* せり　芹　water dropwort *Oenanthe javanica*

shiode しおで　牛尾菜　green brier, cat brier *Smilax riparia*

taranome たらのめ　楤の芽　shoot of the angelica tree *Aralia elata*

tsukushi* つくし　土筆　spore-bearing shoot of field horsetail, sugina (*Equisetum arvense*)

ukogi うこぎ　五加　*Acanthopanax gracilistylus*

uwabamisō うわばみそう　蟒草　*Elatostema umbellatum* var.
majus Family Urticaceae (which contains strawberry nettle and
stinging nettle)

warabi* わらび　蕨　bracken *Pteridium aquilinum* var. *latiusculum*

[yama] **udo*** [やま]うど　[山]独活　(wild) udo *Aralia cordata*

yobusumasō よぶすまそう　夜衾草　a kind of India plantain *Parasenecio hastata* subsp. *orientalis* (formerly *Cacalia hastata*
subsp. *orientalis*). Closely related to **momijigasa**.

yomena よめな　嫁菜　a species of aster *Aster yomena* (*Kalimeris
yomena*)

yomogi* よもぎ　蓬　wormwood, mugwort *Artemisia princeps*

zenmai* ぜんまい　紫萁、薇　Osmund fern, royal fern *Osmunda
japonica*

10 ◆ Soy Sauce

Originally, Japan's basic condiment was **uoshōyu**, a salty liquid
made from rotting fish. Such sauces are still very much in use in
Southeast Asia, but Buddhism, introduced to Japan from China,
brought with it Chinese vegetarianism and a range of basic foods
and condiments based on the soybean. Tofu, miso, and soy sauce
are originally from China. So the fish-based *uoshōyu* was replaced
with the soybean-based **shōyu**, and the Japanese developed such a
highly refined product that no other soy sauce is good enough to
substitute for it.

The early history of soy sauce in Japan is not particularly clear,
but soy sauce seems to be connected with the liquid that separates
from **hishio** and miso during their fermentation. This liquid was
called *tamari*, a word with quite a different meaning from that in
current usage, which means soy sauce made without wheat. This
very early version of *tamari* is now called *tamari shōyu*. The earliest
reference to it seems to be A.D. 775, and somewhat more clearly in
the thirteenth century, but the word *shōyu* doesn't seem to have come
into use until the late fifteenth century at the earliest and wasn't re-

ally established as the name for the sauce until 1643, when the half-wheat, half-soybean product that we know today was developed.

The traditional process of making soy sauce is as follows: grains of whole wheat are parched and cracked and soybeans are steamed. These are then mixed with spores of the mold *Aspergillus oryzae* and incubated for three days, making the **kōji**. This *kōji* is added to a brine solution, the result, now called **moromi**, being put into huge cedar casks holding up to two thousand gallons and left to mature for at least two summers. When ready, the *moromi* is pressed in cotton sacks under heavy weight, a process that extracts crude soy oil as well as soy sauce. The oil rises to the surface and is removed. The soy sauce is pasteurized and bottled. The best quality takes two years to make.

This basic process produces six different types of soy sauce:

1. *Koikuchi shōyu*, heavy soy, is made as above. It is the standard soy sauce, made of 50% soybeans, 50% wheat. If you are going to keep only one kind of soy sauce, this is the one to buy.

2. *Usukuchi shōyu*, thin soy, is used in cooking and is somewhat saltier than *koikuchi shōyu*. The lighter color mainly results from the higher salt content and a shorter period of maturation.

3. *Tamari* is, or should be, soy sauce made without wheat. Because *tamari* goes so well with sashimi, other soy for sashimi is often improperly given this name. Reading the legally required label in Japanese on the back of the bottle can reveal if you are being deceived.

4. *Saishikomi shōyu* is twice-processed soy. For this soy sauce, the *kōji* is mixed not with brine but with *shōyu* and the rest of the traditional process repeated. The product is strong and is especially used with sashimi and sushi. It is often improperly called *tamari*.

5. *Shiro shōyu*, meaning white soy, is a light honey color and has indeed a slightly sweet flavor. The wheat content is much higher than that in the other soys. *Shiro shōyu* should be used as soon as possible after being made since it gradually darkens, though the

taste does not change. It is used a lot in high-class cookery, especially for such dishes as **sunomono**, and has a particularly attractive flavor. Unfortunately it is not available abroad.

6. *Kanro shōyu* is a superior kind of traditional soy made only in the city of Yanai in Yamaguchi Prefecture. It is top-quality, handmade *saishikomi shōyu* with slightly less salt, less **amami** (sweetness), but more *umami seibun*. (*See also* Appendix 14.)

Because the traditional process of making soy sauce takes such a long time, short cuts and quicker processes have been devised, some with atrocious results, some not too bad, but none that can in any way produce soy sauce comparable with the traditionally made product, which now, unfortunately, accounts for less than 1% of soy-sauce production.

11 ❖ Sushi

Sushi is not only one of the best-loved dishes in Japan, but is also extremely popular in many places abroad. It began as a way of preserving fish. This ancient kind of sushi, known as **narezushi**, is not unique to Japan, but is also found in many countries of Southeast Asia. It is not the only feature Japan has in common with those countries, for **uoshōyu**, the forerunner of soy sauce, still made in parts of Japan, has its counterparts in those same countries. The *nam pla* of Thailand is famous.

In Japan the best-known *narezushi* is the **funazushi** of the Lake Biwa area near Kyoto. After the six months or so it takes to mature, the fish is eaten and the rice thrown away, but in contrast with modern sushi, it is not a particularly popular taste.

There are many kinds of sushi, all of them based on sushi rice, which is rice that has been carefully prepared with slightly sweetened vinegar. Sushi vinegar (*sushizu*) is available in bottles. The preparation of good sushi rice takes great skill and experience.

The most highly regarded and no doubt most expensive kind of sushi is **nigirizushi**, also called **edomaezushi**. Edo was the premodern name of Tokyo, and it was there that *nigirizushi* originated and flourished for a long time before spreading to other parts of Japan. *Nigirizushi* consists of a little fistful of sushi rice on top of which some **wasabi** is smeared. On top of this a slice of raw fish or other seafood is placed. Octopus and prawns are cooked, squid is not. Omelet is also used and so are both salmon roe (**ikura**) and sea urchin (**uni**). These latter two are kept in place by a strip of **nori** around the rice. *Nori* is also used to hold blanched **daikon** sprouts (**kaiware**) in place. Among the favorite sushi toppings are **toro**, **ebi**, **shako**, **anago**, **ika**, **tamagoyaki**, and many kinds of raw shellfish. *Nigirizushi* is eaten, preferably in one mouthful, after the topping is dipped in soy sauce.

Osaka's contribution to the sushi scene is **oshizushi**. Sushi rice and seafood, mostly cooked, are pressed in a rectangular box and then cut into slices. Osaka is especially famous for its **battera**, a pressed sushi of mackerel. Kyoto is also famous for its mackerel sushi (*saba no bōzushi*, for which *see also* **sabazushi**), which, however, is not pressed but shaped in a **makisu**. The top quality (but only the top) can be very good indeed.

The *makisu*, which is a mat made of long thin slivers of bamboo for rolling things up, is also and mainly used for making **makizushi**. *Makizushi* is a great standby for almost every occasion, and is not expensive, since a minimum of fish is used, or none at all. Quite thin types of *makizushi* may have just a cucumber filling (*kappamaki*) or tuna (**tekkamaki**). Great fat ones (**futomaki**) are stuffed with **kanpyō**, **mitsuba**, **kōyadōfu**, mushrooms, and omelet, and their very lavishness makes them look inviting. The filling is rolled up in a sheet of *nori*.

Gunkanmaki is a kind of *nigirizushi* in which a topping of **ikura** or **uni** is prevented from falling off by a strip of *nori* around the sides.

With **chirashizushi**, sometimes called **barazushi**, both meaning "scattered," or **gomokuzushi**, literally five-item sushi, the topping is scattered (usually quite artfully) on top of a bed of sushi rice. The color combination is important to make the dish look attractive, so there is usually a sprinkling of **denbu** to add a splash of red. Shredded omelet contributes yellow, and green may well appear in the form of green peas. Chopsticks are needed to eat *chirashizushi*.

Last but not least of the well-known sushis is **inarizushi**. Inari is the fox god, who loves to eat **abura-age** (thin, deep-fried slices of tofu), and *inarizushi* is made by stuffing pockets of sweetened *abura-age* with sushi rice. It is very luscious and moist.

All over Japan there are numerous local varieties of sushi, including such interesting ones as **sugatazushi**, in which a fish is stuffed with sushi rice, sliced, and served in its original shape. This is particularly done with mackerel (**saba**) and sweetfish (**ayu**).

Sushi has an image of delight and gratification among the Japanese. It is great party and picnic food. *Nigirizushi* can be eaten not only in the pleasant atmosphere of a sushi shop, washed down with quantities of green tea, but when the need arises at home to feed unexpected guests, home delivery can be arranged by telephone, and the guests will feel grateful and honored.

12 ✦ Tea

The earliest mention of tea drinking in Japan is A.D. 815, when tea was served to the emperor. This was powdered green tea (**matcha**) and it wasn't until the late sixteenth century that leaf tea, the type known as **sencha**, was imported from China. Leaf tea was easier to make than *matcha* and cheaper, so it became popular. The drinking of powdered tea, which the priests used to keep themselves awake for prayer vigils because it has a high caffeine content, was institutionalized as the tea ceremony. (*See also* Appendix 13.)

Many kinds of leaf tea are drunk in Japan. The Japanese term for tea is **cha**, and the unfermented leaves normally drunk (called green tea, though it is sometimes brown) are referred to with the honorific *o-*, thus *o-cha*. This distinguishes it from *kōcha*, the fermented kind of tea drunk in the West, which is also fairly popular in Japan.

Kōcha is inaccurately translated as black tea, the common English term for the fermented teas usually drunk in the West, even though *kōcha* literally means red tea. To avoid misunderstanding in English, *o-cha* is best translated as green tea, and *kōcha* as tea. *Kōcha* is an imported product, whereas *o-cha* is locally grown, especially near Kyoto and in Shizuoka.

The top grade of green tea is **gyokuro**, which is very expensive and savored in small quantities. Very young buds of old tea bushes specially protected from the sun are used, and the tea is brewed at quite a low temperature, 50°C, in a small teapot known as **kyūsu**.

The middle grade of *o-cha* is **sencha**. Carefully picked young, tender leaves are used for this tea, which is brewed in a *kyūsu* and drunk in small quantities to savor rather than quench the thirst. The water should be 80°C and the tea should be steeped for one minute. *Sencha* is not a breakfast tea but a tea to serve to guests. There is a *sencha* ceremony, but it has never been so widely practiced as the **matcha** ceremony.

The everyday tea is **bancha**. This is the tea to drink at breakfast, the tea to quench one's thirst. It is coarse and full of twigs and is made from older leaves than the other varieties. It is made with boiling water and its flavor is considerably improved if the tea is parched, in which case it is called **hōjicha**. When brewed, *hōjicha* is more or less the color of fermented teas and has a slightly smoky flavor that comes very close to teas drunk in the West. People drink it right up to bedtime as it seems to have less caffeine than other teas. It is quite delightful when made with plenty of leaves.

Genmaicha is another kind of *bancha* that is very good and aromatic. Grains of rice (**genmai**) that are roasted until they pop are added to this tea. It too is made with boiling water and has a slightly nutty flavor.

There are many other "teas" not made from the tea plant *Camellia sinensis*. Kombu seaweed gives **kobucha**, which often has the addition of **umeboshi** and **shiso**. Infusions of **shi'itake** and **matsutake**, bought as powders, are delicious, and *mugicha*, infused from parched barley (**mugi**) and chilled, is the essential cool drink for summer. Many other twigs and leaves, such as persimmon leaves, are dried and infused for their medicinal properties. They are bought at the pharmacy rather than from the tea merchant.

Last but not least, there is cherry-blossom tea (*sakurayu*), an infusion of salt-pickled cherry blossoms. This is drunk on happy occasions, such as weddings, because of the auspicious imagery of the cherry blossom.

13 ◆ The Tea Ceremony

The tea ceremony, *chanoyu* (literally tea's hot water), was brought to Japan as a Buddhist ritual by the Japanese priest Eisai (1141–1215), who had learned about it in China while he was studying Buddhism there. He also brought back seeds of the tea plant.

From its earliest days, the ceremony was associated with Zen Buddhism and was practiced as one of the Zen "ways," as those disciplines are called. In this context it was the "way of tea" (*sadō* or *chadō*). The great Zen monk Ikkyu (1394–1484) thought that tea produced greater enlightenment than long meditation. And indeed the very high caffeine content of powdered green tea (**matcha**) was certainly taken advantage of to keep the monks from dozing off during religious exercises.

The tea ceremony is still an important practice in Zen temples. However, it needs neither temples nor priests, so it often seems to the unenlightened observer purely social. It certainly has an established place in Japanese society as a social activity. No doubt this is connected with the fact that Zen is more a mystical philosophy than a religion, and in any case the link with Zen can be weak. A fuller account of the tea ceremony is given in Kodansha's *Japan: An Illustrated Encyclopedia*.

The meal served at a full-scale tea ceremony (*chaji* 茶事) has an important place in the sphere of Japanese food. This meal (**cha kaiseki**) has had a surprisingly great influence on the West as inspiration for *nouvelle cuisine* and *cuisine minceur*. Apart from *chaji* there is a greatly simplified version called *chakai* 茶会 (tea party), when no meal is provided, merely tea made from the powdered green-tea leaves. Some kind of sweetmeat (**wagashi**), usually **higashi**, is served beforehand.

Although there is a tea ceremony of **sencha**, normally tea ceremony refers to the service of powdered green tea (*matcha* or *hikicha* 挽き茶, 碾き茶). Before the green tea is drunk, sweetmeats, *wagashi* of some kind, often *higashi*, are always eaten to counteract the bitterness of the tea.

14 ◆ Umami and Flavor

Flavor is a complex perception, drawing together the senses of taste and smell, as well as mouth feel, which is the basic element of texture.

There are several striking and very appealing aromas or smells for which Japanese food is notable. Above all, they are associated with soups. The following ingredients—**katsuobushi**, **yuzu**, **matsutake**, and miso—produce some of the aromas or smells unique to Japanese food.

When *katsuobushi*, which is dried, smoked, and cured bonito, and a basic of the Japanese cuisine, is freshly shaved and made into stock, it gives off an intriguing, unforgettable, and highly complex aroma that is clearly related to the smoking, drying, and curing of fish. It is not a marine or fishy smell, but one in which oak smoke predominates.

Yuzu is the Japanese citron. For the most part, only the peel is used, as an aromatic (**suikuchi**), especially in clear soups, the stock for which would be made with *katsuobushi* and kelp (**konbu**). Clear soups are served in lidded bowls, which means that the delicate citrus aroma of the *yuzu* is concentrated under the lid and bursts forth in a stimulating way when the lid is removed.

Matsutake (*Tricholoma matsutake*, formerly *Armillaria edodes*) is a fungus with a striking phallic shape that is the cause of much ribaldry. These fungi grow in pine woods and are difficult to find. In the market they are very expensive. In *Japanese Cooking: A Simple Art*, Shizuo Tsuji writes of them: "Scented with the fragrance of piney woods, these mushrooms that grow only in the wild in undisturbed stands of red pine are so highly prized that they tend to be used as the main ingredient or the primary focus of a dish." The aroma of *matsutake* is incomparable and is perhaps best appreciated in the Kyoto specialty called **dobinmushi**, in which *matsutake* is served in very delicate stock in little individual teapots. The aroma is held in the pot and bursts forth when the lid is lifted.

When the fermented-soybean paste known as miso is made into a soup with either *katsuobushi* or dried-sardine stock, it gives off a strongly savory, appetizing aroma highly reminiscent of roasting meat. This meaty savoriness is typical of fermented-soybean products and is to be attributed to the high quality and quantity of protein-forming amino acids that they contain.

Whereas *yuzu* and *matsutake* are known almost exclusively for their aromas, *katsuobushi* and miso, besides their characteristic smells, also have equally appealing tastes. Both are rich in what is called *umami seibun*, the "tastiness" factor, which is considered, above all in Japan, to be one of the primary tastes: sweet, sour, salty, bitter, and **umami**.

Western science has traditionally identified four basic tastes: sweet, sour, salty, and bitter, with appropriate taste receptors on different parts of the tongue, though the discreteness of the different receptors has now come into question. The Far East, on the other hand, has traditionally favored the notion of five basic tastes: sweet, sour, salty, bitter, and hot (pepper hot). These five have been referred to in Chinese literature from at least the third century B.C. However, in present-day Japan, the fifth one, hot, has been replaced by *umami*, which, it is argued, is one of the basic tastes, with its own taste receptors on the tongue. According to Japanese thinking hot joins "metallic" and "astringent" as one of the three tastes that stimulate the mucous membranes of the mouth as well as the taste buds.

Umami seibun (the tastiness factor) is identified quite specifically with certain amino acids and nucleotides, namely monosodium glutamate (MSG), sodium inosinate, and sodium guanylate. There is no question that, on the one hand, these three are important flavor enhancers and, on the other, have a powerful synergistic effect on each other, up to eight or nine times the properties of the single ingredients. What is hotly disputed, at least outside of Japan, is whether *umami* constitutes a basic taste. Opposing the concept of *umami* as a basic taste would mean opposing the Ajinomoto company, one of the world's largest and most powerful food companies. That company was founded to market monosodium glutamate, which the company called Ajinomoto, "the foundation of taste." The controversy is largely over theory. The practical details concerning these amino acids and nucleotides are, however, important and useful.

Monosodium glutamate is naturally present in many foods, but above all in kelp (*konbu*) and Parmesan cheese. Green tea is pretty high in monosodium glutamate and so is fresh tomato juice and many other foods. The list is seemingly endless.

Sodium inosinate is above all found in *katsuobushi* and in the little dried sardines (**niboshi**) that are used with kelp to make **dashi** stock. Since there is an eight or ninefold enhancement of flavor when these two are used together, it is obvious why stock made in this way should be so effective as the basis of soups, sauces, and dips. This combination also turns up very effectively in Worcestershire sauce and its Japanese derivatives. All this was discovered and put into practice long before anyone knew anything about amino acids.

Sodium guanylate is especially abundant in dried **shi'itake** mushrooms, so it is reasonable, in the light of current knowledge, for vegetarians to use dried *shiitake* instead of *katsuobushi* for making stock. This is exactly what Buddhist vegetarians have traditionally done. Guanylate is found primarily in mushrooms, but there is also a little in beef, pork, and chicken.

In recent years there has been considerable controversy over the use of monosodium glutamate as a food additive, with the problem of the so-called Chinese-restaurant syndrome. The problem is not clear-cut, and there are many factors to consider. Monosodium glutamate as an additive is not a natural derivative of kelp, but is made from sugar-beet molasses or glucose by a process of bacterial fermentation. Whether this is significant is hard to know. At any rate, it is not a "natural" product. An important question is whether there are people who suffer from the monosodium glutamate that occurs naturally in so many foods. Such people would not only have to avoid Japanese soups and stocks, but also such things as soy sauce, which has its own naturally occurring monosodium glutamate.

Perhaps the important factor is the amount of the additive used. It seems clear that many Chinese chefs, especially at cheaper restaurants, are very heavy-handed with their MSG. It is interesting that no one ever complains about a Japanese-restaurant syndrome. Certain it is that an enormous amount of MSG is used in Japan. As well as restaurant chefs, many housewives wouldn't be without it. There are many products available in which an appropriate amount of MSG is combined with salt. The presence of salt effectively prevents one from overdoing the MSG. The Ajinomoto company even markets a superior combination, in which sodium inosinate is added in the correct amount for the full synergistic effect with the glutamate. The main ingredient, of course, is salt. If you are going to use these additives, this is certainly the best way to do so.

Whether glutamate, inosinate, and guanylate, as the "*umami* factor," comprise the fifth basic taste, or whether they should be considered primarily as flavor enhancers, is a theoretical question. The fact is that they do behave as very effective flavor enhancers when used in small amounts and correct proportions.

As for the other tastes, salt and sugar as sweetness par excellence are used as flavor enhancers in Japanese cuisine. Salt, apart from anything else, is essential to the human body. The Japanese diet used to be far too salty, but of late the role of salt as a flavor enhancer has been encroached on by sugar to the extent that virtually all prepared foods sold in supermarkets and convenience stores have at least a little sugar in them, often a lot.

Sour is not a big taste factor in Japanese cuisine, and salt pickles are far more widespread than vinegar pickles. Japanese rice vinegar, as the representative of sour, is very delicate, the best of all being that made from unpolished glutinous rice (**genmai mochigome su**). Sweetened vinegar is used very effectively as a light dressing for such vegetables as cucumber.

Bitter is a very restricted taste anywhere in the world, since it is not a taste humans take to naturally and is generally associated with medicine. In Japan the traditionally eaten guts of some fish and shellfish have a certain bitterness, but in general there is a strong tendency to shun the bitter taste. Such foreign things as bitter chocolate and bitter lemon soft drink have never become popular in Japan, yet other bitter drinks such as beer, whisky, and coffee have all become extremely popular. Chocolate in Japan is another example of the general tendency to sweetness, and avoidance of the bitter, with plain (bitter) chocolate not being at all popular and milk chocolate being far sweeter than would be usual in Western countries.

Japanese food has a reputation for being rather bland, yet despite "pepper" hot not being a major taste factor, it certainly has an important place. **Wasabi**, which is very pungent, is very highly regarded. It is mixed into the dip for sashimi, is an essential ingredient of **nigirizushi**, and has many other uses. Chili pepper is the major ingredient of the seven-spice mixture called **shichimi tōgarashi**, *tōgarashi* being the Japanese word for chili pepper. This mixture is sprinkled on noodles and various other dishes. Then there is **sanshō**, Japanese pepper, the seedpods of the prickly ash. It is also used in the seven-spice mixture. Curry too, as served in the popular *karē raisu*, can sometimes be hot.

As for the "metallic" and "astringent" tastes, they are not really a factor in food.

15 ✦ Vegetarianism

Vegetarianism in Japan is almost completely an aspect of Zen Buddhism, which seems to observe the Buddhist strictures against eating fish, fowl, or flesh ("sentient" creatures) more strictly than other groups. Secular vegetarianism exists, but even the largest cities have little to offer in the way of vegetarian restaurants. Moreover, and perhaps surprisingly, it is not easy to select a completely vegetarian meal at an ordinary Japanese restaurant. Certain Zen temples, however, serve vegetarian food of the most elaborate and delicious kind, and sometimes in the shadow of such temples, non-temple vegetarian restaurants provide the same kind of food.

Shōjin Ryōri

Buddhist vegetarian cuisine is known as **shōjin ryōri**, and was brought to Japan by the monks who introduced Buddhism in the sixth century. *Shōjin ryōri* spread considerably in the thirteenth century, with the arrival of Zen. The most obvious feature is the use of soybean products instead of fish and meat. Soybeans are even used, along with **shi'itake** mushrooms and **konbu**, in making **dashi**. Tofu, miso, **shōyu** (soy sauce) are all great standbys. In Kyoto **yuba** (soy-milk skin) is added to the list, as well as **fu** (wheat gluten). Great importance is given to **gomadōfu**, made of sesame and **kuzu**. It is a very nutritious food and if carefully made by hand, quite ambrosial to eat.

It is a characteristic of Japanese *shōjin ryōri* that the food should not emulate non-vegetarian dishes but be presented for what it is without disguise. There are no "tofu steaks."

The best introduction to *shōjin ryōri* must surely be to eat at one of the many **yudōfu** restaurants surrounding Nanzen-ji, a great Zen temple in Kyoto. Chosho-in is one of them and is actually a charming old temple, quite small, with a beautiful Japanese garden. A platform juts out into the carp-filled pond, and to sit there with a little brazier (**shichirin**) eating *yudōfu* on a calm, sunny day in autumn, especially when the maple and ginkgo leaves are just turning color, is quite enchanting. And memories of Kyoto's *shōjin* food can be prolonged with a *shōjin bentō* bought on the Shinkansen platform at Kyoto Station. It contains over twenty different food items.

Fucha Ryōri

When the great Chinese Zen patriarch Ingen, who gave his name to **ingenmame** (kidney beans), brought his own particular sect of Zen to Japan, he built Manpuku-ji, a temple with a very Chinese-style monastery at Uji, just outside of Kyoto and very famous for its growing of tea. He came to Japan in 1654, and the name of his sect is Obaku *shū* 黄檗宗. Obaku is now also the name of the district within Uji where the temple is.

The Obaku sect's vegetarianism is very Chinese in style, and is called **fucha ryōri**. In *fucha ryōri*, the number of people must be four, or a multiple of four. Two diners face another two diners across the table and eat from common dishes with four portions arranged on them. The basis of the menu is two soups and six dishes of different types (*nijū rokusai* 二汁六菜). There is a serious attempt at making the food look like the forbidden meats and fish. The names of the dishes reflect this and are still Chinese, but over the years one Chinese feature of the food has been adapted to Japanese taste, for it is not so oily now as it originally was. Apart from at the main temple of Obaku Manpuku-ji, this food may be eaten in several temples in Kyoto. Kanga-an, a small convent in Kuramaguchi-dori, is especially charming.

Fucha ryōri is the vegetarian version of *shippoku ryōri* 卓袱料理, a Chinese style of cooking that came to Nagasaki at the beginning of the Edo period and included the flesh of wild animals, birds, and fish.

Caution: Vegetarian visitors on a budget should be aware that temple vegetarian food does not come cheaply. Serving it is a great source of monastery revenue. The meals are no more expensive than a similar level of meal would be in the secular world, but for a real treat at an affordable level, the *shōjin bentō* mentioned previously is the perfect answer.

16 ✦ Wasabi

Fresh **wasabi**, *Wasabia japonica*, the real thing, though grown in Taiwan and New Zealand on a small scale, is scarcely available outside of Japan, though it is sometimes exported frozen. Even in Japan, it is an expensive luxury. What *is* widely available is a green powder which, when mixed with water, is made up into a paste that goes under the name of *wasabi*, a cheap substitute in fact. The best *wasabi*, wild *wasabi*, grows high in the mountains in cool, clear, shaded, shallow streams of spring water. It is also planted on the banks of such streams and is cultivated in fields, especially in temporary vinyl greenhouses built on rice fields idle between the seasons.

All of the plant is used as food. The root, green in color, is grated and mixed with the soy-sauce dip for sashimi. Grated *wasabi* is also put between the rice and the fish of **nigirizushi**. Several kinds of grater are used for grating *wasabi*. The best kind, used by professionals, is made of the skin of angel shark (*Squatina nebulosa*), *korozame* in Japanese, glued onto a piece of wood. However, these are rather expensive, since the sharkskin wears out quickly, so a grater of tinned copper is often used instead. Domestic *wasabi* graters are pottery, metal, or plastic. They have a flat surface with raised teeth but no holes. *Wasabi* should be grated from the top of the root (near the leaf stalks) downward.

Because fresh *wasabi* is expensive, its presence is a good indicator of the better class of sushi shop or restaurant. Though pretty "hot," it is not so harsh as white horseradish, a fellow member of the Family Cruciferae. Fresh *wasabi* does not retain its freshness very long and should be used up promptly. Only a small amount is dried and made into a powder. The powdered version, mixed with water and made up into a paste like mustard, is "Western" horseradish, *Armoracia rusticana*, with green coloring and some mustard powder added. Tubes of prepared *wasabi* are available and may contain both fresh *wasabi* and the made-up powder, or may consist entirely of either one. The one made of *wasabi* only is about twice as expensive as the others, and has a much shorter "use by" date. Outside of Japan, the *wasabi* in tubes is the best choice. An opened tube should be kept in the refrigerator and used up quickly.

An excellent pickle (**wasabizuke**) is made with *wasabi*, and the leaves of the attractive plant are made into a very refreshing vinegar pickle (**suzuke**) and are used in other ways in cooking.

Wasabi seems to lend itself to a considerable amount of commercial deception, possibly because horseradish is called **seiyōwasabi** (Western wasabi) or **wasabi daikon** (wasabi radish). The Japanese are reasonably aware of this, but abroad the true nature of the product often appears only on the label in Japanese, and many people think they are eating *wasabi* when actually they are eating colored horseradish.

17 ✦ Wasanbon Sugar

Wasanbon is a very rare kind of sugar, also called *wasanbon tō*, since *tō* means sugar in Japanese. It is made by hand according to a two-hundred-year-old traditional method, in Tokushima Prefecture, near Kochi Prefecture, on the island of Shikoku.

On the northern border of Tokushima Prefecture, an unusual kind of sugar cane, *Saccharum sinense*, Chinese sugar cane, is grown. In Japanese it is called *take kibi* or *chiku sha*. It is quite thin, being less than half the thickness of ordinary sugar cane, *Saccharum officinarum*. It is harvested in December and January, and the sugar production begins in the middle of December.

First, the cane is crushed to extract the juice, which is boiled until a lot of the water has evaporated and it reaches the "soft ball" degree. The resulting syrup is cooled and poured into pots to set. It is now called *shirashita tō*, consisting of crystallized sugar and invert syrup (molasses, treacle).

A lengthy process now begins, the purpose of which is to remove every trace of the treacle. It is in this process that techniques not used elsewhere are employed. Only about a third of the *shirashita tō* is sugar, treacle comprising the other two-thirds.

To extract the treacle, the *shirashita tō* is wrapped in cloth and placed in a pressing box that is operated by means of levers and heavy stones tied to ropes. This is followed by *togi*, literally "washing," which is actually a process of hand-kneading with water for two hours. Traditionally the pressing and washing were done three times, hence the name *sanbon*, *san* meaning three. Nowadays it is actually done four times, the sugar getting cleaner all the time as more and more treacle is removed. It is believed that the thoroughness of this process is the reason for the softness and fineness of this sugar. When the pressings and wash-kneadings are finished, the sugar is laid out in trays for a week's drying. Altogether the process takes twenty days.

The product is an extremely fine sugar that has a very important place in the making of top-quality **higashi**, a candy-like confection used in the tea ceremony. The top-grade makers, mostly in Kyoto, which is famous for *higashi*, say they cannot use any other sugar.

Higashi consist of a mixture of rice flour and fine sugar pressed into decorative molds and colored to suit the design. Their appearance can be very attractive, whereas their flavor is simply the flavor of raw rice flour and sugar. Since the flavor of *wasanbon* is so smooth and its sweetness so delicate, it is easy to understand what an advantage these qualities give to the *higashi* made from it. In any case, *higashi* are very convenient for drinking **matcha** (tea-ceremony tea) to sweeten the mouth in readiness for the bitterness of the powdered green tea, since most of them keep forever and can be permanently on hand for whenever needed.

Recommended Reading

Following is a select list of reading recommended by the author.

Japan Travel Bureau. *Illustrated Eating in Japan*. Tokyo: Japan Travel Bureau, 1985.

> Don't be deceived by the small, trivial appearance of this book. It is extremely useful and utterly reliable. An absolute mine of information; just what you want to know.

Krouse, Carolyn R. *A Guide to Food Buying in Japan*. Tokyo: Charles E. Tuttle, 1986.

> Full of useful information, this is the book to take shopping with you.

Okura, Shunji. *Japanese Cuisine*. Takamatsu: Cécile, 1993.
大倉舜二 『日本の料理』高松、セシール、1993.

> Bilingual English and Japanese. Although this book can be obtained only from the mail-order firm that published it, it is well worth doing so. It covers a very wide scope from the historical and cultural points of view, and is full of the most wonderful and informative color photographs, since the author is a photographer.

Richie, Donald. *A Taste of Japan*. Tokyo: Kodansha International, 1985.

> Quite the best book for an introduction to Japanese food in context. Interesting, well-illustrated, and accessible.

Tsuji, Shizuo. *Japanese Cooking: A Simple Art*. Tokyo: Kodansha International, 1980.

> An outstanding book, not only for its very wide range of reliable, fundamental recipes, but also for the enormous amount of useful, accurate information about Japanese foodstuffs, their availability abroad, and what, if anything, to substitute. It is not surprising that M.F.K. Fisher should have agreed to write the introduction.

Yoneda, Soei. *The Heart of Zen Cuisine: A 600-year tradition of vegetarian cooking*. Tokyo: Kodansha International, 1982. First published as *Good Food from a Japanese Temple*.

The kind of book one falls in love with, it is actually very practical. Zen vegetarianism is very important in Japanese food culture and this book takes you to the heart of it. The introduction by Robert Farrer Capon is not to be ignored.

Yoshida, Mitsukuni and Sesoko Tsune. *Naorai: Communion of the Table*. Hiroshima: Mazda Motor Corporation, 1989.

Sheer delight, it is my favorite book on Japanese food. It has just the right historical and geographic perspective, is beautifully illustrated from old books and paintings as well as with excellent photographs, and is interesting and very informative. I have to recommend this book because it exists and is extremely good. I also reluctantly have to point out that it is out-of-print and unobtainable.

Works of Reference

IN JAPANESE:

石毛直道、辻静雄、中尾佐助、全巻監修『朝日百科、世界の食べもの日本編』全4巻、朝日新聞社、1982–83

上田万年　ほか編『新大字典』講談社、1993

『食材図典』小学館、1995

『調理用語辞典』全国調理師養成施設協会、1986

日本魚類学会編『日本産魚名大辞典』三省堂、1981

『平凡社大百科事典』平凡社、1984

堀田満　ほか編『世界有用植物事典』平凡社、1989

益田一　ほか編『日本産魚類大図鑑』全2巻「本文、図版」東海大学出版会、1984

森雅央　ほか編『新編日本食品事典』医歯薬出版株式会社、1982

本山荻舟著『飲食事典』平凡社、1958

Richard Hosking holds an M.A. from Cambridge and is professor of Sociology and English at Hiroshima Shudo University. He has lived in Japan since 1973 and has lectured on Japanese food at the Oxford Symposium on Food and Cookery, the Symposium of Australian Gastronomy, and elsewhere throughout the world.